December 1997.

To: Nana.

Happy Christmas

With love,

Ross, Ryan & Tom
xox

Follow That Bird!

Follow That Bird!

Around the world with a
passionate bird-watcher

Bill Oddie

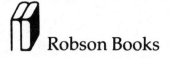 Robson Books

This Robson paperback edition first published in 1997
First published in Great Britain in 1994 by Robson
Books Ltd, Bolsover House, 5-6 Clipstone Street, London
W1P 8LE

Copyright © 1994 Oddsocks Limited

The right of Bill Oddie to be identified as author of this
work has been asserted by him in accordance with the
Copyright, Designs and Patents Act 1988.

British Library Cataloguing in Publication Data
A catalogue record for this title is available from the
British Library

ISBN 0 86051 919 8 (hbk)
ISBN 1 86105 088 7 (pbk)

Printed by The Guernsey Press Company Ltd, Guernsey,
Channel Islands

Contents

Introduction

I was taking part in the Great Kenyan Bird Race in December 1987. We were on our way to Malindi in a tiny plane, being buffeted all over the place by a thunderstorm. It was pretty scary. Suddenly, out of a flash of lightning, an enormous raptor loomed in front of the cockpit window. It looked ominously like the Angel of Doom. But it wasn't. In fact, it veered away into the clouds before we could identify it. All fear vanished, as the cry went up:

'FOLLOW THAT BIRD!'

We did. The incident provided a Martial Eagle for our list, and a title for this book. It also seems to encapsulate what a weird and wonderful hobby birding can be.

This is a collection of 'traveller's tales' of the pursuit of birds. When I started, I expected it to consist of a large number of short chapters. It has ended up as half a dozen long ones. This is because, as I wrote and remembered, I was constantly reminded of how much more there is to bird-watching than 'just' the birds. There are the places, the people, the time in your life – maybe even in 'history' – the thoughts and the emotions. It all contributes to what some of my birding friends call 'the value', what the Irish call 'good crack'. Sometimes – like the Kenyan eagle – it verges on the surreal. It can also be silly, serious, sad, and even a little bit sexy!

I've enjoyed recollecting and reliving. I hope you enjoy reading. I also hope you're inspired to get out there, and 'do it yourself'.

Good birding, and may you never dip out.

1
Sites for Sore Eyes
Morocco

A true story. A bird-watcher was in love. He asked his sweetheart to marry him. She said 'yes', and eventually 'I will'. She was not a bird-watcher. They discussed where they should go for their honeymoon. She said she'd like to go somewhere warm but, being considerate – and realistic – she appreciated that it would be nice for him if wherever they went also had a few birds he could watch. He was grateful, whilst assuring her that bird-watching would most certainly be purely incidental on this trip. They settled on Cyprus in the spring. They arrived at their hotel, late in the afternoon of a beautiful balmy day in May. That evening, they enjoyed a romantic supper on the terrace. As they sipped their retsina and nibbled their kebabs, he barely noticed the flock of two hundred Bee-eaters circling above them, distracted as he was by the sparkle in his true love's eyes. The song of a nearby Great Reed Warbler was utterly drowned by her seductive whispers. Love is truly not only blind but also deaf, to all but the overwhelming promise of imminent passion. The setting sun bathed them in an irresistibly erotic glow as they rose from the table and moved towards the bridal suite. At the door, she paused. Not reluctant, but teasing, knowing that every second of delicious delay would merely heighten the bliss of eventual consummation. She nuzzled his ear: 'Join me in five minutes. I'm just going to slip into something more....' She replaced the adjective with a smile that implied more than he'd ever dared imagine. He was left on the balcony to wait. Five minutes ... to listen to his own heartbeat, to scan the stars, to smell the scented air, to smile at the moon, and to anticipate the moment when he and his lover would be reunited in the most meaningful – and, by the sound of it, extremely saucy – way. He looked at his watch. Half a minute to go. To pass the time he started counting the pebbles in the garden. One of them appeared to wink at him. A Nightjar perhaps. No ... but it was surely a bird. Barely ten metres away. He couldn't resist it. He tiptoed towards it. It didn't move. He knelt and picked it up. He recognized the species immediately. It was dead, but in perfect condition. An immaculate specimen, worth keeping, if only as a memento of the most special of all nights. A night that was about to reach its climax.

'You can come in now,' she called.

He opened the door. The room was almost in darkness and yet the scene was gloriously and unashamedly visible. The lace curtains flapped gently at the window. Through them, the filtered moonlight directed an enticing spotlight inexorably towards ... the bed. The quilt was turned back. The sheets were silk. And ... there lay the lady. Her hair was spread out across the pillows, and she was spread out everywhere else. The diaphanous black négligé, which she had bought specially for this night, she had draped across her limbs so that it concealed just enough to be utterly, tantalizingly revealing. Her arms were loosely at her sides, but, as he gazed at her, she turned the palms of her hands upwards in the subtlest yet most irresistible of invitations. It was a moment she had planned for months, maybe years, maybe all her life.

'Well?' she whispered, and closed her eyes, awaiting his response. When she opened them again, he had disappeared. He was in the kitchen.

'I'll be with you in a minute, darling, I'm just skinning a Short-toed Lark.'

Well, OK, maybe I've added a few touches of the Barbara Cartlands – or was it Jackie Collinses? – and maybe it wasn't Cyprus, but it *was* a Short-toed Lark and, basically, it *did* happen. I presume the story was related by the wife to the lawyers, as grounds for an instant divorce. Or maybe it was the bird-watcher's defence.

'Oh come on. surely you can appreciate my dilemma? A perfect specimen of a Short-toed Lark. I mean, I know it was *dead* and it wasn't going to fly away or anything but, if I'd left it, it could have gone off. It was a very warm night, and the fridge hadn't been switched on, so I couldn't put it in there. And, be honest, she did look as if she was set for quite a long session, and, anyway, I usually fall asleep afterwards and then I wouldn't have got round to skinning it till next morning. And, let's face it, even if I had just left it by the side of the bed and got on with the "business", I know I wouldn't have been able to concentrate. I'd've just wanted to get it over with so I could get back to the lark. Or I might not have been able to do anything at all actually, and she wouldn't have been very happy about that, would she? I mean, I did go back in as soon as I'd finished skinning it, but she said she found the lark's blood under my fingernails really off-putting. And I did try and make it up to her next morning by bringing her breakfast in bed, but unfortunately I'd forgotten I'd put the corpse in the yoghurt pot, 'cos it was the only thing I could find that was airtight. She didn't have to keep screaming like that, though. It isn't as if she took a bite out of it! Anyway, I reckon I could divorce *her* for withholding my conjugal rights. I tell you, that was the only lark I had on *that* honeymoon!'

Now I dare say that you are expecting me to confess at this moment that *I* was that bird-watcher, and that the lady was my ex-wife. But no. Believe me, if it had been me, I wouldn't be telling you about it. So why did I relate that story? Well, merely to illustrate that bird-watchers can be pretty obsessive, perhaps to the point of grotesque insensitivity, and certainly to the point of neglect of spouses and children. There are plenty of birding widows and orphans, but I hope that *my* wife or children would not complain that they are amongst them. I like to think that I've got things reasonably in proportion. By way of some kind of evidence in support of this claim, I offer the fact that we often manage to share family holidays – something which I know some birders and their families find almost impossible to do. The birders feel unbearably constrained if they are not constantly allowed out birding, and the families feel understandably neglected if they are constantly being left. The answer, of course, has to be a compromise, something which, alas, birders seem to find harder to achieve than families. That I think I *have* achieved it myself, I admit, owes a great deal to the fact that I have a very tolerant wife (Laura) and daughter (Rosie), who also have enough sense of self-preservation to know that I would be totally unbearable if I were not unleashed now and again.

For what it's worth, a quick guide to sharing happy holidays for birders and non-birding families would involve some of the following tips:

From the non-birding woman's point of view, probably the most efficient solution would be to marry a man so tedious that you have no wish to spend any time at all with him on holiday anyway. Then you'll be positively grateful if he keeps going off bird-watching. The problem is that you'll probably go off him pretty rapidly as well.

So seriously folks.... This advice is aimed at the birders. (Usually male, though I'm not really sure why.) Make sure you go somewhere nice, at a time when the weather is going to be warm enough to spend time on a beach or in a pool (or even the sea, if you want to risk it). Decisions on what is 'nice' in terms of place and time must involve a ruthless degree of honesty from the birder. A windswept promontory with a sewage farm and a power-station on it might well be great for birding, but not for sunbathing. Even Cyprus – or any other Mediterranean country – isn't guaranteed to be 'good for sunbathing' if you go too early in the spring. As a general rule: if it's 'just right' for a bird-watcher, it's too cold for the family. Conversely, if it's 'just right' for the family, it's probably too hot for birding. The way to please everyone is to go to a hot country but rise early, when it's still cool and, as it happens, the birds are most active. Go birding for a few hours, but try to get back when the family are getting up. Then spend the day *en famille* and – if you can bear it – without binoculars. At the end of the day, nip off for a brief evening excursion, but make sure you're back in time to organize the evening meal, which should be taken fairly late, and with plenty of wine, so that everyone sleeps in the next morning. Except, of course, *you*, who have to be up at dawn to go birding again. And so on. If possible, also plead for one 'big day out' each week. You could trade this off for a 'big day out' for the family, doing something you probably don't really want to do, like looking at markets or ruins. Keep an open mind, and you might even find you rather enjoy these things. You might even come to realize that there's more to life than birds!

This is all perfectly serious advice, and I hope it may be of help. The really important thing is that, on a family holiday, on no account should you have a check-list of species you are determined to see. Listing and twitching instincts must be suppressed, otherwise you and everyone else will suffer. By all means keep a holiday 'log', as it were, but, in my experience, the route to sanity and satisfaction is to regard wherever you happen to be as your temporary 'local patch'. Find a likely looking area, preferably within walking distance or a short drive from the hotel or villa, watch it every day, and see what turns up. Well, that's what I do, anyway. Plus, I always get a file full of gen from Steve Whitehouse's Foreign Bird Information Service, just so I can make the most of any 'big days out' I manage to negotiate.

This was how I approached Morocco. Easter fell early in 1994, so that if we were going to get a week away somewhere 'nice' – and guaranteed to be warm – we were going to have to migrate pretty far south. As it happens, the end of March is a time when many birds should be migrating north, and since Morocco also has a reputation for being one of the world's most productive birding destinations, I was pretty confident that a good time could be had by all. I had already checked the maps and site guides, and accepted that there was no way that I would be able to cover the distances between the various hot spots. Organized birding teams, hell-bent on ticking off all the Moroccan specialities, take at least ten days and rack up enormous mileages – not to mention petrol bills – as they travel from the marshes of the north to the deserts of the south, via the mountains in between. Laura, Rosie and I were going to be staying, for one week, at a town called Taroudant, about an hour's drive inland from the seaside resort of Agadir. According to my Foreign Bird Information, Taroudant was ornithologically noteworthy only for the fact that Little Swifts nested in the town – not, as it happened, a species I 'needed'. There were a couple of other sites fairly close by, but any expeditions to the edge of the Sahara or the peaks of the High Atlas were clearly well beyond the range of even the biggest day out. Long before we set off, I had quite happily come to terms with all this, and had, in fact, set myself a limit of a two-hour driving radius. It honestly didn't bother me that there were lots of species that I knew I wouldn't see. I was looking forward to finding myself a 'local patch' and hopefully enjoying some migration, and also to enjoying a relaxing week off work. I had only one worry – pestering.

The Moroccan guidebook hadn't helped. The very first paragraph seemed designed to put people off:

> Prepare for a culture shock ... there is a hardcore of young males whose sole aim in life appears to be the exploitation and harassment of the tourist.... You WILL be harassed, there is no doubt about it. The intensity of the hustling depends on a combination of factors such as your sex, your age, your dress and appearance, your location and the opportunity you present as a potential victim.

What exactly did that last bit imply? 'The opportunity you present....' Like, you should be OK as long as you don't go out! As it happened, only a few days before we left I'd been talking to a couple who had just returned from ten days in Marrakesh, during which time they had never managed to get further than the front steps of their hotel. I tried to console myself. My friends were undeniably and obviously well off. Sunbed complexions and gold watches – they might as well have had 'potential victim' tattooed on their foreheads. Moreover, they were in Marrakesh, which is famous for hassling. Taroudant, however, according to the same guidebook, was reputedly much less frenetic and threatening; 'Marrakesh with manners', it was dubbed. And in any case we had carefully chosen to stay at a hotel advertised as being so sedate and elegant that Laura and Rosie wouldn't mind being imprisoned there for a week, if that's how it turned out. Of course, I, on the other hand, would go totally bonkers. Mind you, as a fifty-year-old bearded male, dressed in grotty shorts, tatty T-shirt, and a Suffolk Wildlife Trust baseball cap, I surely wasn't a prime hassling target. Or was I? I would soon find out.

Meanwhile, we landed safely in Agadir, picked up the hire car, drove the hour or so to Taroudant, and checked into the hotel, pausing only to tick off the Little Swifts that were swirling around in the lowering black raincloud that soon sent us scurrying for the shelter of our room. So far, not so good. The weather wasn't what we'd flown four hours south for, I'd already seen the local rarity, and the room was far from 'sedate and elegant'. It was small and gloomy. Fortunately, a rapid firm complaint to the manager put that right, and we were moved up to a much nicer room – with windows! – and even a little terrace, on which I could shelter under the parasol and enjoy the view of several other little terraces and half a palm tree. It wasn't exactly the great outdoors. It certainly didn't constitute an adequate 'local patch'. After supper, we all went to bed to get an early night, and because it was raining, and because we didn't dare step outside the hotel. Rosie fell asleep instantly, whilst Laura and I consoled ourselves by muttering: 'It will all be better in the morning.'

Eventually, we nodded off. About three hours later we were awake again. It wasn't better. It was worse. But then, it wasn't morning. It was still the middle of the night. The sound that had woken us was the voice of the muezzin calling the people to prayer from the tower of the town mosque. This is what happens in Muslim countries. In a stunningly effective combination of ancient and modern, the traditional chanting is amplified through a sound system that produces enough distorted decibels to drown out a heavy-metal rock concert. (Maybe they get second-hand gear from Guns 'n' Roses.) The effect on a newly arrived British tourist who is not expecting it is truly alarming. It doesn't so much wake as shatter you. However, it is generally considered inadvisable to stick your head out of the window and yell 'Oi! Put a sock in it!

There's people trying to sleep round here!' (I got that tip from the same guidebook.) After half an hour, we'd sort of got used to it and began to drop off again. Then it stopped. After another half-hour, we got used to the silence, and finally fell asleep, still muttering: 'It'll all be better in the morning.'

And soon it was. Morning, and better.

I was woken at about six o'clock by the chirruping of Bulbuls, a song so relentlessly cheery that it could be taken for sarcasm after a rotten night's sleep. I heard Laura mutter something about 'shut those bloody birds up' as I attempted to dress quietly in the dark without waking her, and failed. I fumbled for my binoculars, tripped over my tripod, yelped, apologized, and tiptoed outside. The sky was clear, the sun was rising, and I felt a little frisson of optimism. As I scurried through the grounds of the hotel, I couldn't help but notice that it really *was* rather elegant. The air was already quite warm, and the swimming-pool looked almost inviting. As I passed the restaurant, I noticed fresh fruit had been laid out for breakfast. Laura and Rosie would surely be content enough here. The little pang of guilt I always feel when I'm 'escaping' evaporated, and I headed for the real Morocco, and the answer to the question that was still troubling me: would I be pestered?

I scampered to the car and leapt in, without looking up, in case I caught the eye of any potential pesterers lurking outside the front gates. I needn't have bothered. No one was awake yet. A five-minute drive took me to the Oued Souss. I had already made up my mind that this was a likely local patch. It had looked promising when we'd driven past it on our way in the previous afternoon. What's more, it was mentioned in my site guide gen as being a likely spot for the Red-necked Nightjar and other species.

First, let me describe the area. *Oued* is presumably a

variant of the Arabic for *wadi*, and *wadi* is something else for 'river' or – to be more accurate – 'a dry riverbed'. Anyone who has travelled in North Africa or the Middle East will be used to the fact that wadis may contain everything from bushes to goats to unexploded mines, but they rarely contain running water. Except possibly for about two minutes, on one day, in the middle of winter, after a freak thunderstorm. On that morning in March, I found the Oued Souss to be a quintessential wadi, the way I'd always known them. Dry as a bone. But enormous with it. The riverbed must be nigh on a mile wide, and stretches away either side as far as you can see. It is a huge expanse of sand and long-congealed mud and scattered stones and pebbles, and the whole thing is studded with little bushes, some of which look like – and may well be – tamarisk, while others resemble overgrown lupins. It didn't look like the sort of terrain that could harbour many pesterers. But were there any birds?

I parked by the side of the road and checked my info: 'Red-necked Nightjars may be seen at night' (as long as it's not pitch dark, I presume!). 'They may also be found roosting under the trees in the wadi.'

I love these encouraging instructions in site guides. Is the opitmism in the mind of the writer or the reader? The word is '*may*' be found. You can take this as you would in a holiday brochure: 'You may take a drink on the terrace', meaning it's up to you. The drink is definitely there, all you have to do is take it. So, the optimistic interpretation is: the Nightjars *will* be roosting under the trees, all you have to do is look at them, and tick 'em off.

Or ... you can interpret the 'may' as rather more cautionary, meaning: 'the Nightjars *might* be under the trees' ... or they might not. Such is most birders' optimism – and desperation not to dip out – that I suspect most of us take the site guides as absolute gospel and consider suing the writer if the birds aren't there. In fact, that 'may' ought to be translated even more cautiously. How about: 'One afternoon, about ten years ago, a very lucky bird-watcher happened to be caught short as he drove by the Oued Souss. He nipped behind a convenient tamarisk for a pee, and – by a million to one chance – flushed a roosting Red-necked Nightjar. Even if you can find the right bush – out of the 5,000 that are growing in the riverbed – it is extremely unlikely that the bird is still there. But it *may* be.' Well, it wasn't.

Not to worry, my 'info' offered an alternative site, and not too far away. Meticulously, I followed the directions: 'Half a kilometre towards the town of Taroudant on the main road, an unsurfaced track leads off north. Take this for one and a half kilometres, to where there is a line of tall trees. Opposite this, another track leads down to a rubbish tip.'

I drove back a little way along the road, parked again, and studied the terrain, working out which was north, and estimating one and a half kilometres. Then it struck me that there was only one line of trees on any visible horizon, and OK, maybe it was more like one and a quarter kilometres away, but that *had* to be the place. In any case, they might as well have just said, 'follow the smell!'

Why is it that so many bird sites are totally hideous? God knows, Morocco is full of exquisite scenery. I was even surrounded by some of it. I could see the misty foothills of the Atlas Mountains from where I stood. The nearby orange grove looked cool, and smelt delightfully fragrant. But where did the instructions tell me to go? The bloody rubbish dump. Isn't it always the same? 'Follow the path past the sewage farm, turn left at the pigsties, jump over the septic tank, and the bird may be perched on the rotting cow outside the abattoir.'

I re-read the gen: 'Red-necked Nightjars may be heard

calling from the tall trees, or hunting over the fields at dawn or dusk.' But *not* one hour after sunrise, as it now was. 'Other species in the area may include larks, pipits, wagtails, finches and buntings.'

And where would they be, I wondered? In the sweet-smelling orange grove? Not likely. I could see them right now, flitting about on the festering rubbish tip, totally oblivious to the appalling stench. Ah well. I set off in pursuit of Serins and Thekla Larks, across the ponging peelings and rancid remains. It was so unsavoury that even the mangy-looking dogs that were snuffling around the edges didn't bother to come over and bite me.

Well, one thing's for sure, I thought, I won't be pestered here.

Wrong!

"*Allo M'sieur!*'

I nearly jumped out of my skin.

"*Allo M'sieur,*' he repeated.

Now I speak enough French to be aware that "Allo M'sieur' translates apparently innocently as 'Hallo sir'. A very polite greeting, in fact. Almost reverential. It could perhaps be colloquialized into 'Good morning mister'. Harmless, and endearing even. However, I knew better. When "*Allo M'sieur*' is delivered by a Moroccan youth of indeterminate age – somewhere between eight and eighteen – it is undoubtedly a prelude to pestering. For "*Allo M'sieur*', substitute 'Oi, you!'

He said it again. For the moment, I was struck dumb, trying to work out where he'd come from. The only substantial cover within – was it one and a third kilometres? – was the line of tall trees. Maybe *he'd* been roosting under the tamarisks. I resisted asking him if he'd been sleeping on a Red-necked Nightjar. I resisted saying anything. I just walked away. I know it seems a little ungracious, but that was what the guidebook suggested I do. I just kept staring straight ahead, as his voice faded in my ears, '*M'sieur! M'sieur! M'sieur!*' The tone of urgency and anxiety would have melted the heart of a traffic warden. But I didn't look round. It went quiet. I'd lost him. Then he suddenly popped up right in front of me. How did he do it? Did he have a twin? Was it a camera trick? Now I *did* look behind me. Nobody there. I turned back. Nobody there either. Was I hallucinating? No. "*Allo M'sieur!*"

This time he was almost literally in my pocket.

'*Donnez-moi les cigarettes. Dirhams. Bonbons. Stylos.*'

I considered asking him to state his priorities. Which would he prefer: a smoke, money, sweeties, or pens? On balance, I reckoned the last seemed potentially the least damaging to his health, but I wasn't carrying a pocketful of biros, so I couldn't oblige. And anyway, I remembered the advice in the book: 'How to deal with hasslers. There are various different approaches you may try.' That, presumably, was 'may' in the site guide sense; i.e. none of these methods might work.

'Method number one: completely ignore them. Do not speak and on no account make eye contact. This is difficult, but eventually they will lose patience and go away.' Yes indeed, maybe after two or three hours, or two or three days, or possibly at the immigration desk at Heathrow Airport if they haven't got a visa. If they have, you may simply have to accept them into your family for ever. I gave ignoring about ten minutes, but finally snapped when the lad leapt out in front of my camera just as I was focusing on a Hoopoe. I tried method two: 'reasoning'. This involved trying to communicate in my limited French.

'*Je cherche les oiseaux. Seulement, s'il vous plaît. Laissez-moi. Allez! Allez!*'

This didn't work at all. It wouldn't have got me through

A-level oral, but it was presumably just intelligible enough for him to realize that I must have understood his demands perfectly well. So he repeated them: '*Cigarettes, dirhams, bonbons, stylos.*'

Now that I'd admitted I had a vocabulary, I delved deeper into it. '*Non!*'

Which he countered with: '*Oui.*'

I tried a greater emphasis. '*Non non non non non!*'

To which he replied: '*Oui oui oui oui oui!*'

This was a slightly less interesting exchange than Linguaphone Lesson One, so I tried feigning madness.

Actually, by this time, I wasn't entirely feigning. I started talking to myself, walking round and round in circles, singing extracts from *Little Shop of Horrors*, and even baaing. This was meant to be a satirical reference to the fact that he simply kept following me like a sheep. I don't think he got the point. Whatever I did merely seemed to entertain him. When I made silly noises, he laughed, and when I sang he either applauded or attempted to join in. Presumably he was actually sending me up. He was also sending up most of the birds, and I was getting totally exasperated.

For a reckless moment, I considered the very last resort in dealing with pesterers: give them what they're asking for. Then I remembered the guidebook's advice, written in big black letters and underlined: 'ON NO ACCOUNT GIVE THEM ANYTHING'.

Why not? I wondered. OK, cigarettes I could figure. Bad for young lad's health. Indeed, this boy was coughing his lungs up before my very eyes. *Bonbons*. Bad for the teeth? Well maybe, but, more to the point, I didn't have any on me. Dirhams I did have, but only in the enormous notes that I'd exchanged my traveller's cheques for at the airport. I wasn't going to give him twenty quid, and somehow I doubted if he'd have any change on him. So what about '*stylos*'? Well, actually, I thought Stylos went out years ago, along with nylons and nutty slack, but presumably any pen would do. But all I had was the little pencil I kept stuck in my notebook. My 'shadow' was casting envious eyes at it at that very moment. Then it struck me as to a possible reason why the guidebook suggested I shouldn't give him anything. He might be grateful. Then I'd *never* get rid of him. He didn't seem a bad lad. I suspected that if I handed over money or a pen he might feel that I was purchasing his services for at least the rest of the day. Either he would want to be my 'guide' (round the rubbish tip perhaps?), or he would feel obliged to do my field sketches for me. Nevertheless, I decided to risk it. What could I afford to sacrifice? Not the pencil. Not a 100-dirham note. I fished around in my pocket, and found a packet of slightly mangled indigestion tables that I always carry with me in case of heartburn. I gave him one.

'*Voilà! Un bonbon*,' I announced.

I might as well have broadcast it through the muezzin's PA system: 'Roll up, roll up. Get your sweeties here!'

Within seconds, six more boys leapt out from behind tamarisk bushes, hands grabbing at my pockets: "*Allo M'sieur ... 'allo M'sieur ... M'sieur ... M'sieur ... M'sieur!*'

I fled back to the car, screaming, and pelting the boys with indigestion tablets as I ran. I guess that's what the book meant by presenting an opportunity 'as a potential victim'. Except I wasn't 'potential' any more.

I returned to Oued Souss under cover of darkness and ticked off Red-necked Nightjar. They were indeed calling from the tall trees, and eventually one swooped out over the orange grove, though, to be honest, for all the detail I could see on it it could have been a model aeroplane. Over the following days I continued my morning and evening jaunts. The birding was excellent, and the pestering really not too bad. Or maybe I was getting used to it. Or maybe they were getting used to me. Word had probably gone round the local kids that the bearded bird-watcher didn't smoke, eat sweets, or carry pens or dirhams. Maybe they were sorry for me because I suffered from heartburn. In any event, the "*Allo M'sieurs*' almost began to seem little more than what the words actually meant. I nodded, muttered '*bonjour*', and was generally left alone.

Until my 'big day out'. I spent the morning in the low Atlas, with little more than a herd of goats and a couple of Black Wheatears for company. (Just about the least exciting 'lifer' I've ever had. It's a wheatear, and it's black. Good name, though.) Then I hit the road for a two-hour drive to a major site, the Aoulouz Gorge. I like gorges. We had spent another recent family holiday in Minorca, and my favourite spot there was the Algendar Gorge, where a shady little path wound up between massive crags, with Booted Eagles, Red Kites and Lesser Kestrels swooping out of them, Alpine Swifts circling above, and the bushes along the valley floor alive with flycatchers, warblers and orioles. It was full of life, and yet incredibly peaceful. Maybe Aoulouz would be like that. The little sketch map in the info gen looked very promising. Lots of interesting birds were marked on it. Long-legged Buzzards and various eagles and falcons in the cliffs, migrant warblers in the bushes, and even waders – and real water! – in the wadi. The only comment that struck a slightly suspicious note was that the site was 'best viewed from the P32', the main road. If it was easily accessible to birders, it probably followed that the birders would be easily accessible to pesterers. How true.

As I turned the bend in the road, I could see the gorge up ahead. Beyond it was a rather grubby-looking town, which seemed to consist largely of gloomy grey cement factories. Below it was the river. Relatively full of water, yes, but equally full of people, and lorries and donkeys and cows and dogs, all intent on digging out gravel or throwing in rubbish. Another typical famous bird site! However, the cliffs of the gorge were pretty impressive, and I could well believe that they were the home of various raptors. I had to look. I parked on the bridge, got out of the car, and prepared to be hassled. To my surprise, it didn't happen. I scanned the cliffs, and realized why. Clomping back along a narrow path was a phalanx of bird-watchers, all armed with binoculars, telescopes and tripods. Behind, in front, and all around them were about thirty small boys. From where I stood, I could hear the massed chorus of '*M'sieurs!*' As I got nearer, I realized that this was rather inappropriate, since the bird-watchers were German. But hassling is the same in any language. As the birders clambered back into the coach, the boys hurled themselves at the windows in a final frantic attempt to extract dirhams or *stylos*. I saw my opportunity and raced past the mêlée and up the track, hoping I hadn't been noticed. Five minutes later I thought I'd got away with it, as I stood alone, gazing vertically upwards at a Long-legged Buzzard. Then I heard it call: "*Allo M'sieur*'.

I literally jumped, and, in dropping my binoculars, accidentally clobbered the tiny boy on the head. He laughed. So did I.

This one I liked. For the rest of the afternoon, we wandered up and down the gorge, chatting away in broken French. He even pointed out objects of wildlife interest to me, although I found it hard to feign too much enthusiasm for a squashed centipede and a cow. This time, when I found myself humming with something approaching contentment, he copied the tune, and even tried a few harmonies. At no time did he ask for anything. Which of course made me resolve that, when we got back to the car, I would definitely give him something. Unfortunately, by the time we did get back, the German birding party had gone, thus releasing the other twenty-nine boys. As soon as I appeared with my little chum, they pounced. He was almost flattened in the crush. I clambered into the car with their hands thrust into my face, and not entirely gracious requests for cigarettes and money drowning my protests. I saw my new friend pushed to the back, looking almost on the verge of tears. As I reached into my bag for a couple of coins, the grasping and yelling became even more aggressive. So did I. I parted the crowd with one arm, reached out to the boy with the other, and pressed the dirhams into his hand. '*Pour vous!*' I announced defiantly.

As I closed the door, the other kids kicked it, beat on the windows, and spat at the windscreen. I drove off, with them haranguing me in words that I presume were mildly – or possibly considerably – obscene. Glancing back in my rear-view mirror, I could see my little friend standing at the roadside, clutching his coins and looking rather bemused. I had a horrible feeling I was leaving him to be bullied. It really didn't seem fair. Up to that day, I'd almost felt guilty for being horrible to the local kids, now I was feeling guilty for being nice. As for the boy, he was probably wishing he'd never spoken to me. I had a sad suspicion that he was about to be taught a lesson: 'If they're going to beat you, join 'em.'

On my final morning in Morocco, I set myself a little quest. I resolved to try and take a stroll somewhere where I could guarantee that no kids would run the risk of meeting me. I also wanted to end with a bit of flourish, bird-wise. The previous evening at the hotel, I had been chatting to some English geography students who'd been doing a project in the area over the past couple of weeks. They told me that they'd been studying the geology of a valley only about twenty minutes' drive away. There was a dry wadi, uncultivated countryside (a rarity in the area), some ancient ruins on a nearby hillside and 'lots of birds'. They were sure I'd love it there. The area was marked on the map, but it wasn't listed in my birding site guide. Which meant it might even be quite attractive! It sounded exactly the sort of place I wish I'd found on the first day.

And so it was. I arrived soon after dawn on a wonderful sparkling morning. The narrow road had got even narrower, and become unsurfaced, to the point of threatening my tyres, so I parked and began walking. The 'forest' in this part of Morocco hardly seems worthy of the name. It consists of stony semi-desert, with scattered argana trees. The arganas look like the viciously thorned acacias, but are, in fact, a sort of super-rugged olive, that bear fruits whose 'juice' is used for everything from cooking-oil to back liniment. At a glance, the argana forest doesn't look like a bird-rich habitat but – as I soon discovered – it is. There were lots of migrants flitting around: homely 'British' species – like Whitethroats and Chiffchaffs – as well as the 'locals' – Bonelli's, Subalpine, Orphean and Olivaceous Warblers. As I walked, Tawny Pipits and Short-toed Larks skipped ahead of me, and Black-eared Wheatears flipped up onto their favourite perches, if they weren't already occupied by Woodchats and Great Grey Shrikes. The morning air was 'chinging' with the calls of Bee-eaters, and then, soaring right through them, came a majestic male Montagu's Harrier. This was what holiday birding was all about. I'd found my 'local patch'. A pity we were flying home next morning!

Never mind. I put such thoughts out of my head as I scaled the hillside to explore the ruins. There had to be something up there. Indeed there was; a fantastic panoramic view, for a start. The cultivated fields of the Souss valley stretched away to where they met the Atlas Mountains. The morning was so clear that I could even see the snowy caps of the highest peaks. Much closer – in fact hardly half a mile away – the sun was glancing off a tiny patch of water. There, blinking incongruously in the middle of this semi-desert, was a 'reservoir', no bigger than a tennis-court. A sandgrouse drinking-pool, if ever I saw one. At that moment I could see only a swirl of swallows over it, but I had a feeling that I would be proved right before the sun was much higher. Meanwhile, there were small birds flitting around the ruins. Within the next five minutes, I'd had three 'trip ticks': a Black Redstart, a couple of Trumpeter Finches and – best of all – a quartet of Ortolan Buntings. They were definitely not local breeders; these were real migrants, just stopping off to rest on the ridge on their way north. I focused on them as they posed on top of a prickly pear, with a backdrop of the valley beyond. I was aware of a few farmers and goatherds making their way out into the fields, but they were away in the distance. I was completely alone. Me and the birds. My dream come true. Then it was shattered.

"*Allo M'sieur!*"

Where on earth had he come from? I was in the middle of the wilderness. Or was I? I realized that the so-called ruin I was perched on was, in fact, the dilapidated garden wall of a small farmstead which – being built in local stone – melded so completely into the hillside that it was almost perfectly camouflaged. I suddenly felt I was trespassing, as indeed I may well have been. It struck me that the boy might have been sent to check me out. His next words seemed to indicate just that. Instead of demanding money, he asked me what I was doing.

'*Que faites-vous?*' he said (or words to that effect).

I told him: '*Je cherche les oiseaux.*'

'Ah!' He replied and, seemingly satisfied that I was not scrumping prickly pears, he went away. I was completely gobsmacked. This didn't happen in Morocco. Much to my utter astonishment, I had been left alone.

I carried on down the hillside, musing that this was

indeed my perfect morning. As if to celebrate it, a small squadron of Black-bellied Sandgrouse wheeled across the path in front of me, on their way from the drinking-pool. Oooh, isn't it lovely when you're proved right? I felt gloriously smug. By this time the sun was getting warmer, the migrants getting dozier, and my stomach getting emptier. Laura and Rosie – who'd had a lovely week – would just about be getting up. Time to go back and join them for breakfast. This was the bird-watching/family holiday system in perfect working order. And no pestering!

I spoke too soon. I was just about to get back into the car, when the familiar cry echoed across the valley: '*M'sieur! M'sieur!*'

It sounded more urgent than ever. I turned to see the little boy who had asked me what I'd been doing racing towards me. Had his father sent him back to get me? He'd probably been given a lecture: 'You did what? You just asked him what he was doing and ... left him alone! You're a disgrace to the family. Get back there and pester him immediately, or you're no son of mine.'

'*M'sieur! M'sieur!*'

He was getting closer, yelling, and waving frantically. I was really disappointed. I'd told him I was bird-watching and he'd gone away. I thought he'd understood. Or maybe he had. I suddenly realized what he was on about.

'*M'sieur! Les oiseaux!*'

'*Oiseaux*'. He was running over to tell me about some birds. My faith in Moroccan youth was instantly restored. Maybe he just wanted to make sure I'd seen the Sandgrouse. Or perhaps he'd just spotted a Rufous Bushchat in his garden – I really wanted to see one of those. Then I realized he was holding something in his other hand. Maybe he'd caught a Rufous Bushchat! Perhaps he was birder himself, a ringer even, with a couple of mist-nets set up against the prickly pears. He panted up to me. I was intrigued enough to ask: '*Oui? Qu'est-que c'est?*'

'*M'sieur. Voilà. Les oiseaux.*'

He held out his hand. In it was – not a Rufous Bushchat – but a clutch of three rather scrawny baby pigeons. They barely had quills on them. In fact they barely looked alive. '*Les oiseaux,*' he repeated.

I nodded and smiled weakly. I didn't 'need' domestic pigeon for my trip list. He offered them to me. What was I supposed to do with them? He pointed at the birds, then pointed at my mouth, and explained.

'*Mangez!*'

I was hungry, but not that hungry. I pleaded for the pigeons' lives as best I could, though my French seemed utterly inadequate to the task. I burbled on about '*Retournez au nid*' and '*Cherchez la mère*', and so on. As I drove away, I left the lad looking perplexed, perhaps even a little hurt. He was still feebly brandishing the pigeons, and calling after me in words I simply couldn't understand. It was only when I was halfway through breakfast back at the hotel that it struck me: maybe I'd just dipped out on the first Moroccan breeding record of Rufous Turtle Dove! What's more, the boy's family were probably frying them at that very moment.

2
Simply the Best
Scilly

SCILLY SEPT. '74. (mainly).

HOOPOE — (If you see it - you're lucky!).

St Mary's

imm Sabines Gull (when you see one - you know!

At sea!

wet... mystery warbler

Lavatory Brush (for comparison).

St Agnes

BONELLI'S WARBLER (concealing most relevant features).

St Mary's

SERINS (at least there were three). (...at least!)

cloak the short wings.

MELODIOUS WARBLER

St Agnes

St Agnes

AQUATIC WARBLER (beware confusion with small tiger). 'showing well' in my dreams!

SOLITARY SAND. Tresco

Birdwatcher with dry feet....

SPOTTED SAND.

'Wot! No Spots'

Tresco

St Mary

8 TICKS

Distant DABCHICK in the rain, impersonating Pied Billed.... or were there two birds?......

2 mysteries....

In this kind of book – what do they call it? A 'miscellany', or an 'anthology' (no, that sounds far too poetic for me) ... er, 'bits and pieces about birds' ... well, you know what it is, 'cos you're reading it – anyway, in this kind of book, it would be positively perverse of me not to include a chapter on 'My Most Memorable Bird Holiday'. It would be equally peculiar if I managed to avoid mentioning the Isles of Scilly (or 'the Scillies' or just 'Scilly', which is apparently the 'proper' title ... says who?). Wouldn't it be neat and convenient if the two topics happened to coincide? Well they do! If only life were always so well structured.

First of all, a few basic Scilly facts (if you know all about it, feel free to skip to next paragraph). The Scillies are a group of islands about 30 miles south-west of Cornwall, which is, in turn, the most south-westerly county in Britain. The archipelago consists of literally hundreds of little islets and rocks, but there are five inhabited islands: St Mary's, St Agnes, St Martin's, Tresco and Bryher. None of them is very big. St Mary's is the largest, and it is the only one that has proper roads, cars, buses, and even a policeman. Nevertheless, you could still walk right round it in a day. The biggest choice of accommodation is on St Mary's, but, even if you stay there, you will inevitably go 'island-hopping'. Twice a day, a small fleet of boats offers a water-taxi service to the other islands – none of them is more than half an hour away. Each island has a different character and look to it; all are delightful. What's more, the beaches are as vast and sandy as any in the world, the seas are crystal clear and safe for bathing, and the rock pools are teeming with life. All in all, Scilly is the perfect destination for a family holiday. End of travel commercial.

Scilly also happens to be arguably the most productive birding destination in the British Isles, especially if you are turned on by rarities. The only problem is that everybody knows it. October is *the* month. The so-called 'Scilly Season' has, in recent years, been featured in newspapers, magazines, books, and on television and radio. The media simply adore the invasion of twitchers with their mobile phones, CB radios and pagers. No doubt the Scilly boatmen, British Airways Helicopters, and Cornish charter-plane companies adore it, too. And so do the hotel and boarding-house owners, whose holiday season is extended by an extra month. And, I presume, thousands of birders adore it as well, or they wouldn't keep going. Personally, I don't know if I adore it or not. I've never dared try.

I've been to Scilly many, many times over the past thirty years, but the last time I was there in October was a long time ago. It wasn't a relaxing experience. Although the number of birders on the islands was nothing like what it is nowadays, St Mary's was almost full. Well, at least, that's what it felt like to me. I spent one day there. Every time I thought 'Ah, I've got this bit to myself', I'd turn a corner and bump into another birder asking, 'Anything about?' Every time I raised my binoculars, people would come galloping from over the horizon yelling, 'What have you got?' Such encounters ought to be an opportunity for cheery co-operation but – own up – they're not. They are, in fact, incredibly tense. Logically, anyone asking 'Anything about?' or 'What have you got?' *should* be hoping that you will reply with the name of a rare bird. But do they *really* want that? In fact, if your response is 'No' or 'Nothing', they seem positively relieved. Any other answer, and they'll go into shock or panic:

'Where is it? Is it still there? Will I see it if I run there now? Will you come with me and show it to me? Will you carry me? If we don't see it, will you tell me it was stringy in the first place, and you're withdrawing the record? On second thoughts, can we pretend we never met?'

On that day on St Mary's, I decided that the least traumatic policy was to say nothing. So if anyone asked if there was anything about, I said exactly that: 'Nothing.' It wasn't deceitful, because in fact that's precisely what *was* about that day. Nothing. At least, that's what the other birders told *me*. But then, maybe they'd decided they couldn't stand the stress, either.

By now, it may have dawned on you that the reason I appreciate the psychology of a twitchy mentality is that, to a point, I have exactly that myself. Or, at least, I certainly did back in those days. In fact, I think my attitude may have been particularly insidious. I loved seeing rare birds. Most of all, I loved finding them. So I tried to go my own way, and not merely follow the crowd. However, if I *did* find a rarity, I was happy to tell other birders and 'grip them off'. But I hated being gripped off myself, and I also hated to dip out. The truth was that *I* was the one who couldn't resist asking 'Anything about?' or 'What have you got?' and *I* was the potential panicker. I'd managed to get through a day without dipping, but there was simply no way I could do my own thing and ignore the other birders. Unless I got away from them altogether. So I did.

I went to stay on Tresco. I lasted nearly a week. I had the mornings and evenings to myself, and spent most of the days avoiding the daily boatload from St Mary's, even to the extent of going back to bed or locking myself in my room. I figured that what I didn't know, I couldn't miss. Meanwhile, I resolved to find my own birds on the island. There were two flaws to this plan: the first was that there weren't any rare birds to be found; the second was that this didn't stop me claiming I'd found one.

I shall always plead 'exacerbating circumstances'. It was early morning, in poor light, and it was raining, and the bird was swimming around half hidden amongst the reeds, on the very far side of Tresco Great Pool, and it kept diving 'in a funny way'. Nevertheless, it was a Dabchick, *not* an immature Pied-billed Grebe. My reputation would not have been so tarnished had I 'suppressed' it. Instead, I actually sat smugly on the quayside waiting for the St Mary's boat to come in, so I could announce my discovery. Everyone raced off to the Great Pool to scan the reeds. Fortunately, the bird proved so elusive that most of the visiting twitchers saw nothing. One of them did see a Dabchick. To his eternal credit, he discreetly took me aside and enquired softly whether I was 'entirely sure about the Pied-billed Grebe?' It was nice of him to be so sensitive. Or was it just my good luck that he found me on my own? If the rest of the day's birders had been there, would he have announced loudly: 'It's just a bleedin' Dabchick, you stringer!' Anyway, he left me with my telescope and my conscience. I used them both. First, I found the undeniable Dabchick; then, I quashed any pathetic temptation to try the old 'two-bird theory' (i.e. that there was a Dabchick *and* a Pied-billed Grebe on the pool, but they were never visible at the same time), and finally, in a fit of positively masochistic humility, I actually ran round the island finding as many birders as I could and admitting I'd made a silly mistake. Amazingly, perhaps, no one mocked me to my face, though no doubt they did behind my back.

Or maybe they understood. I said I made a 'silly mistake'. Perhaps that should be a 'Scilly mistake'? Not just a bad pun, but a medical condition. Maybe it's a certifiable syndrome amongst birders who try to stay on one island and find their own birds: they start hallucinating. (Come to think of it, I reckon it's happened before, and since – and on Tresco too – though the people involved are far too distinguished for me to name them here!) Anyway, back in that October, some of the St Mary's lads obviously decided that I had to be lured away from Tresco as quickly as possible, either for my own good or, possibly, for theirs, so that they didn't have to keep chasing after my dodgy sightings. This was way back in the days before pagers and portables, but there were good old-fashioned telephones. Thus, one evening, came the call to the New Inn (where I was staying). 'Bill, you must come over to St Mary's tomorrow. We've got Little Bunting, Rose-coloured Starling and Red-eyed Vireo.' Every one a 'lifer'.

Next morning, I took the first boat over. I spent the whole day wandering round St Mary's in pursuit of the birds. I missed the lot. I arrived at the Bunting field to be told: 'It flew off half an hour ago.' I moved on to the Starling trees: 'It was here earlier.' On to the Vireo hedge: 'Not seen today.' I trudged round the circuit again. It was the same story: 'You should have been here ten minutes ago.' Or ten minutes later, or maybe not at all, thank you very much. I made one last desperate attempt at individuality. Marching purposefully away from the packs of doleful dippers or grinning grippers, I set off for a remote, under-watched bit of the island where, as far as I knew, no one had looked that day. I looked. I saw nothing but, as I wandered back towards the town, a frantic twitcher staggered past me. Clearly a man in pursuit of a rarity. I had to ask.

'What is it?'

'Olive-backed Pipit at Pellistry.'

Where I'd just come from! It was only a mile or so back, but I carried on walking, straight to the airport. I caught the next chopper back to Cornwall, and the next train home.

So ... Though 'my most memorable birding trip' *was* to
the Scillies, it *wasn't* in October. It was in September 1974.
Blimey, that's going back a bit isn't it? Does that mean I
haven't had a really good trip for twenty years? No,
there've been lots of good ones, but none of them could
match this one for – how can I put it? – 'completeness'.
There's more to the really memorable trips than just the
birds. Some of my birding mates call it 'value', the Irish
call it 'good crack'. It's to do with the company, the
atmosphere, the ambience, and the time in your life,
maybe even in history – it all comes together. It's hard to
sum up, but I will tell you about it.

First of all, I have to admit that although the birds might
not be everything, they are – let's face it – jolly important!
On this trip, they were spectacular. Well, they were to me
at the time. This is an important element. Back in 1974 I
had a healthy life-list, but I was hardly a member of the
'400 Club'. (I'm still not. Not by a long way.) I still
'needed' several not-incredibly-rare species, the sort of
birds that some twitchers might mock a little, but are still
scarce enough to appear on Birdline. You can decide for
yourself whether to deride or admire them as they occur.
Some I think you may even envy a little. Anyway, the plain
statistical fact is that during a nine-day holiday, I had eight
'lifers' – almost one a day. The account that follows is
unashamedly 'birdy' (I'll get to the extra value later!). If
you're not into this sort of vicarious pleasure, I apologize,
but most birders – despite our competitive nature – seem
to be strangely generous-spirited when it comes to reading
about other people's best days – or weeks – so I hope
you'll enjoy it.

On 6 September we arrived in Cornwall. 'We' being
Andrew Lowe (a long time birding companion of mine),
Robin Hemming (a friend of Andrew's), and myself. In the
afternoon, we just had time to nip into Marazion Marsh,

which is conveniently situated just near enough to the Penzance Heliport to be a consolation if your flight is delayed. Although it can be equally frustrating if you've heard of a good bird there and your flight is on time, so you haven't got time to race along and see it. The secret is, of course, to build a little Marazion time into your schedule. Either by luck or judgement, we had half an hour. There were two rather nice birds there: a Grey Phalarope and a Black Tern. Neither exceptionally rare on their own, but a rather odd and somewhat significant combination. You don't often see the two together, because Grey Phalaropes tend to be blown in by strong westerly winds, whilst Black Terns arrive on easterlies. The wind that day was blowing strongly from the west, but the Tern was evidence that it had been from the east pretty recently. We boarded our helicopter, optimistically predicting that Scilly could well have birds from both directions. Our optimism was soon confirmed.

We arrived on St Mary's too late in the day to do any birding, but we did make one phone call, to David Hunt. David was 'the man on the spot'; indeed, that was what he called himself in his little adverts in *British Birds* or *Birds*, the RSPB magazine (which were, incidentally, the only bird magazines in those days). Having worked on the islands as a gardener and various other things, he had, relatively recently, set himself up as a guided-tour leader. Most of his clientele were 'beginners' or holidaymakers, and most of David's days were spent pottering along with a crocodile of luminous anoraks in tow, with him pointing out Turnstones and toilets, rather than 'little brown warblers'. Nevertheless, he was in the field an awful lot, and therefore found plenty of rare birds. He was also the only source of 'recent reports and news' for any visiting birders. Not that there *were* many visiting birders; 'I think there may be one or two around,' he told us. Well, there *may* have been one or two, but as it turned out, we didn't see any of them until later on in the week. Just think about that the next time you're stuck at the back of a 1,000-plus queue, waiting for your 10-second turn to tick off the latest twitch ... a week in Scilly in September without seeing any other birdwatchers! Ah, but did we see any birds? You bet. David pointed us in the most promising direction, and next morning off we went.

DAY ONE

Early morning at St Mary's Airport. As anyone who's been there will confirm, the airfield is not completely flat. At first glance, the short-cropped turf may look devoid of birdlife, but round the edges there are various little dips and hollows in which rarities can hide away, whilst indulging their fantasies that they are really pottering around on the Arctic tundra. I always feel a bit mean disillusioning them. I apologized to the Dotterel, whilst attempting a Norwegian or Scottish accent to make it feel more at home. We then descended towards Porthellick Pool, where a Spotted Sandpiper (from America) was reported to be in temporary residence. We had barely left the airport perimeter when the bird flew up the hill to meet us. It settled on a peaty little puddle and allowed us to tick off the checklist of identification features. It even called, which 'difficult' waders normally refuse to do, unless subjected to harassment, prayer or bribery. This one merely received our thanks. During the rest of the day, we appreciated the healthy numbers of more common migrants – Pied Flycatchers, Whinchats and Wheatears – whilst also ticking off two more of David's tip-offs: a Woodchat Shrike and an Iceland Gull. So already, that was one 'lifer' for me (the Spotted Sandpiper), and good birds from all points of the compass. All to ourselves.

DAY TWO

Early-morning rain had cleared up in time for us to catch the ten o'clock boat to Tresco. The fact that there are five visitable islands is one of the delights of Scilly. It can no doubt also be one of the frustrations, if you're on the 'wrong' one when your pager bleeps or your mobile phone rings, and you hear news of a rarity on one of the others. But, back in 1974, there were no such agonies to be suffered. We arrived at every new island full of anticipation as to what we might find. There was no information service telling us 'not to bother'. Whilst the rest of our boatload toddled off to take tea in the Tresco Gardens, we checked out the waders on the Abbey Pool. There were a couple of Little Stints, a Greenshank, and a Common Sandpiper, to compare with yesterday's Spotted. Then, we walked across to the eastern end of the Great Pool. Here there is a sort of shallow extension of the main lake, largely cut off by reeds, and with a narrow strip of muddy shore along it. The far bank is more or less inaccessible to people, and is therefore much beloved of dozing ducks and shy species such as crakes or rails. As I scanned it, a Water Rail shuffled out. I was enjoying the view when Andrew suddenly leapt in front of my binoculars, gesticulating urgently. He literally nearly knocked me over. I had long since learned that this violent behaviour was a good sign. He'd got something (apart from an attack of St Vitus's Dance!).

'A Sandpiper ... just flew across.'

We scanned the distant shore.

'There's a Common,' I announced.

'No, not that ... There! Just beyond the Common, half hidden in those stumpy reeds.'

He was right. It certainly was a sandpiper. I stared at the bird and offered an identification.

'It looks like a Green.'

Andrew lowered his binoculars and relished the drama of the moment: 'It hadn't got a white rump.'

I knew what he was implying. The Green Sandpiper has a big white rump, and is a fairly common bird. The Solitary Sandpiper *looks* like a Green, but *hasn't* got a white rump, and is a very rare bird.

So Andrew had caught a very fleeting glimpse of it in flight and declared: 'It hadn't got a white rump.' The question was, now that it was feeding along the distant shore, had it *still* not got a white rump!? It was impossible to see. We all lay down and propped our telescopes on our knees. There were none of these new-fangled lightweight 'spotting scopes' in those days. As for carrying a tripod, we'd've as soon worn a skirt and a liberty bodice. We used three-foot-long phallic symbols that Nelson would have been proud of. For what seemed like an hour we lay there till, at last, the Sandpiper stretched its wings and flashed its delightfully dark hindquarters. We had chronic neck ache, but we also had a Solitary Sandpiper. At the time, it was only the seventh British record. Amazingly, almost exactly a year later, on precisely the same bit of mud, I found the eighth!

Meanwhile, back in 1974 ... I still needed a Melodious Warbler....

DAY THREE

And on St Agnes, I got it. Not one Melodious Warbler, but three. Keeping up the 'lifer-a-day' routine. And keeping up the 'west and east' principle, there was a Pectoral Sandpiper paddling around in a marshy little pool close to where the warblers were guzzling blackberries.

Back at St Mary's Airport in the evening, the Dotterel had been joined by a Buff-breasted Sandpiper. This species has become much scarcer in Britain in recent years, but in the seventies it was a regular on Scilly each September. I even knew American birders who flew over specially to see them, as they are hard to find in the States away from the Canadian Arctic, where they breed. I rather like the idea that the US field guide lists Buff-breasted Sandpiper habitat as: 'The Arctic tundra, and St Mary's Airport and Golf Course.' (It doesn't really.) Some years small flocks built up on the island – I think the most I ever saw together was thirteen! Meanwhile, one was enough.

DAY FOUR

We spent the early morning saying hallo to the Buff-breast, the Spotted Sand and the Woodchat. Then we gathered on St Mary's quay to meet David Hunt. He had arranged a very special boat trip. We were going to go shark fishing. Admittedly, when David had phoned us the previous evening, we'd been less than enthusiastic. We were clearly 'on a roll' with the birds, and were loath to interrupt our run by wasting the day going fishing. It seemed particularly unlikely that I'd get my daily lifer on board a 20-foot catamaran. Then David explained that the boats often attracted seabirds and, with the recent westerlies, there might be a chance of Sabine's Gull. This had become a 'bogy bird' for me, as in twenty years' sea-watching I had never seen one. It was certainly worth a try.

I should point out that this was long before the days of large organized 'pelagics' on big stable ships, with nice solid railings along the side where you can lean with your binoculars, or even balance your 'scope. The *White Hope* was not the ideal boat for bird-watching. It probably wasn't the ideal boat for shark fishing by the time we'd all clambered on board. There were, as I recall, about eight of us. Four fishermen, including the skipper, and four bird-watchers, plus the assorted equipment for both activities: rods, lines, buckets and bait, binoculars and cameras, as well as fuel for ourselves and the boat. There wasn't much room for any sharks we might catch, but we didn't let that bother us as we sailed out of the harbour. Personally, I couldn't believe there really were any distant cousins of 'Jaws' swimming around out there. Surely this was all a ruse to relieve a few would-be Robert Shaws of their money? – 'Come to Sunny Scilly. Enjoy a Cornish Cream Tea, and Land a Great White.' Oh sure.

About four miles east of the islands the skipper dropped anchor and distributed the rods. The fishermen dangled their lines over the side, whilst the bird-watchers scanned the horizon. In no time at all we'd spotted a couple of 'large' Shearwaters, living up to their name and shearing over the water. Unfortunately, they were way off on the horizon, so we couldn't be absolutely sure of their identity. Mind you, they looked a bit different from one another, so they went down as 'probably Great and Cory's'. Which no doubt they were (though we didn't bother to discuss which was which!).

So far, not bad, but not the close-up views we'd almost been promised. Nor, indeed, the sharks the fishermen had hoped for. At this moment, the skipper addressed both problems. He produced the 'chum'. This is the shark bait. Sweet name, 'chum', isn't it? It's sometimes called 'rubby-dubby', which is also a charming name. Both are ironic euphemisms for a bucketful of rotten fish guts that smell even worse than they look. Sharks love chum. So do seabirds. In fact the seabirds got there first. No sooner had the first sloosh of rancid giblets hit the water than terns appeared from over the horizon, swarming round the boat like bees round a honeypot ... or, indeed, seabirds round chum. The terns were pursued, almost inevitably, by a couple of Arctic Skuas. They actually chase the terns so that they'll cough up the horrible stuff, which means that it's not only rancid, it's also regurgitated. And that apparently makes it even more delicious to a Skua. Soon after the Skuas came a little posse of Storm Petrels and, close behind them, a couple of Leach's Petrels. This was getting good.

Then it got better. Over the waves came bouncing a small gull with a dark forewing. It was heading straight for us, so much so that we couldn't actually see the wing markings properly. Was it just an immature Kittiwake? Well, the basic flight pattern of juvenile Kittiwake and Sabine's Gull are indeed very similar. I defy any sea-watcher to deny – hand on heart – that he hasn't strung the odd 'Kitti' in his time ... even if his conscience got the better of him before he actually claimed a Sabine's. I know I'd done it several times over the years. I also knew I had never seen a Sabine's – until that moment. Someone had once told me: 'When you see one, you'll know.' And I did. There was just something about that flight 'jizz'. It wasn't a Kittiwake – more like a Little Gull in fact – but it was, without doubt, a Sabine's. And to prove it, it flew right up to the boat, landed on the water, and let us photograph it. In case we needed a second opinion, another one joined it a few minutes later.

Then the sharks started biting. They weren't Great Whites; they were small Blues. Well, the first one wasn't very big – it can't have been more than a couple of feet long – but it was undeniably a shark, with those glazed eyes and vicious teeth. I certainly felt it belonged more in the water than flapping and snapping around by our feet, which it did until the skipper bonked it on the head. So there really *were* sharks out there. I was surprised and a little alarmed. Robin was inspired and challenged. Being relatively new to birding, he'd had about twenty 'lifers' on this trip already and probably felt satisfied. He'd done the birds, he was ready to try the fish. In fact, he looked well suited to the job. He was a strapping lad, with a bushy beard and a woolly hat, a budding Ancient Mariner if ever I saw one. We immediately appointed him as a one-man team, to represent the birders against the anglers. It was no contest. No sooner had he flung in his hook, than he was reeling in a shark. And another. And another – each one bigger than the last. He soon became convinced that there was a real monster out there with his name on it, and he was determined to land it.

I shall never forget the moment that he did. It was one of those times in life when everything coincides in a climax of exquisite chaos. The great writers of farce work years to achieve it; if it had been a scene in an Ealing comedy it would have become a classic. First, there was a slight lull in the proceedings. Everything had gone a bit quiet. The wind had dropped, the clouds had rolled away, and the sun was shining. Most of the birds had gorged themselves on chum, and lolloped off over the waves with bulging bellies. The fishermen had gone sullen with jealousy at Robin's success. The birders were relaxing smugly. Andrew was sunbathing and snoozing; David was changing film in his camera and polishing his telephoto lenses; and I was gazing at the prow of the boat as it slowly rose and fell with the swell. Now that the excitement had died down, I was slowly beginning to admit to myself that I felt terribly seasick. I began to edge across the deck to get to an appropriate throwing-up place. Then all hell broke loose. Robin suddenly yelled 'I've got another!' and began frantically reeling in his line. This woke up Andrew, who blinked at the sky and shouted 'Long-tailed Skua!' He wasn't dreaming. As if from nowhere, the bird suddenly materialized, circling right above our heads. Andrew leapt to his feet. David frantically fumbled with his lenses, trying to get his camera gear back in active condition. I dived for

my binoculars with one hand, whilst covering my mouth
with the other. At which moment Robin gave a mighty
heave and a six-foot shark landed right in the middle of the
lot of us. I didn't know whether to scream, be sick on it, or
jump overboard – I think I achieved a combination of all
three. The skipper leapt forward and started lashing out at
the thrashing tail and jaws with a huge wooden club. The
boat rocked to and fro. I'd love to have had a 'long shot' of
the whole scene. Shark flailing, skipper bashing, fishermen
cowering, me honking, David juggling, Andrew bird-
watching, and Robin grinning. 'Fade to black', as they say
in the movies.

DAY FIVE

We woke to a wind change. It had gone south-east. Up at
the Golf Course, the effect was immediate: a Tawny Pipit
on the tenth fairway.

So what was today's 'lifer' going to be? We took the
boat to St Agnes. The conditions were very promising
indeed. All morning, there was a light drizzle. Then, about
midday, the rain stopped and the sun peeped out. So did
the birds. We were clearly witnessing a small 'fall'.
Whinchats perched on the fence-posts, Pied and Spotted
Flycatchers flitted along the hedges. A Wryneck suddenly
hopped up onto a dry-stone wall. The previous day's
Melodious Warblers were matched by a couple of
Icterines, giving the opportunity for comparing wing
lengths and head shapes. Everywhere we scanned some
little migrant would pop out and then disappear into the
bushes. There had to be something good with them. And
there was. But not for long. I think I spotted it first. Clearly
a *Phylloscopus* warbler, but 'that's not a Chiffchaff' I
muttered, as it perched on a bramble about twenty yards
away. I got Andrew on to it. Neither of us was offering an

instant identification. Instead we started making notes: 'Chiffchaff-sized. Grey upperparts. Wings a little darker. Clear white underparts. Thin white eyestripe, dark eye. No yellow on it at all!' Until it flew. Which it did after about forty seconds, revealing a slightly paler rump with a tinge of yellowish in it. Andrew and I spoke at once: 'Bonelli's.' I don't think either of us had ever seen one at that time, but we knew what they were 'supposed to look like'. But do you ever *really* know a species till you've seen it?

The warbler in question was never found again. This wasn't entirely surprising; small birds can very easily lose themselves in the maze of hedges in the middle of St Agnes. Moreover, as the weather cleared up, the birds cleared out, and, by the time we left the island, there was hardly a migrant to be seen. Back on St Mary's, we rang David Hunt and told him we'd had a Bonelli's. I could sense that he was sceptical. 'What colour were the legs?' he asked, challengingly. We had to admit that, as the bird had been static amongst brambles, we really hadn't seen the legs clearly. This was undoubtedly a weakness in our description, but our sighting was nevertheless accepted by the British Birds Rarities Committee. However, I can now admit that for some years I harboured just a tiny sneaky little doubt about that Bonelli's. Until I saw another one. It happened to be in the Canary Islands, though it was also in September. For a moment, instead of Lanzarote, I was back on St Agnes and I was watching *that* warbler. It *was* a Bonelli's. Five days – five 'lifers'.

DAY SIX

Was spent mostly chasing round the brackeny slopes and bulb-fields on the far side of the Golf Course in pursuit of a very flighty Hoopoe – 'lifer' number six. This was another of those birds that had eluded me for years. Twitchers call them 'blockers', which is a dreadfully anal expression. They even talk about 'unblocking'. Still, I suppose I'd rather be unblocked by a Hoopoe than a pound of senna pods.

DAY SEVEN

A day off – for the birds, anyway. Heaven knows, we tried. We revisited the Tawny Pipit and Woodchat, and paid our respects to a couple of Pectoral Sandpipers that had settled at Porthellick, but no 'lifer'. Never mind, there's always tomorrow.

DAY EIGHT

And indeed there was. It started well, on St Mary's Golf Course. The Hoopoe decided to strut around at our feet, instead of leaping over the horizon. The Tawny Pipit had found a friend. The airport Buff-breasted Sandpiper had changed location and started a flock ... of two. And there were two Dotterels as well.

It was obviously 'National pairs day'! As we docked at St Agnes, we were greeted by two Roseate Terns, and there were two Wrynecks along the wall. Maybe I'd get two 'lifers', to make up for yesterday's blank. I suppose, in a way, I did. Unfortunately, the first one didn't count. It looked rare enough: a passerine of some sort, feeding in a weedy field. Yellowy body, with a read head and pale beak. Red-headed Bunting, perhaps? No. A Tanager from America, maybe? No. It was a Weaver Bird from a cage, actually.

We moved on to the area round the chapel, where we'd glimpsed our Bonelli's. There were a few migrants, but nothing like what we'd seen on our previous visit. We decided to try 'the big pool'. Despite its name, St Agnes

Pool has only a small area of open water. This is very shallow, and can be good for waders or crakes. Round the water, however, is a wide fringe of fairly low tussocky reeds. At a glance it doesn't look as though very much could hide in there, but in fact it is much denser, and much better cover, than it appears. I have learnt from experience that, unless you gently walk through the reeds, you can miss all sorts of things. Pipits, wagtails and buntings are all fond of lurking in there, chuckling at timid birders who don't want to get their feet wet. So are some warblers.

At first, I thought this was going to be another Bonelli's-like experience. As we approached the pool area, a little brown bird shot out from by an overgrown wall and dived into the reeds. It could have been a Sedge Warbler, but it didn't seem 'quite right' to me. It seemed rather too yellow. By this time, I was getting quite cocky: 'I'm sure that was an Aquatic,' I announced. My confidence was totally unjustified, since I'd never seen an Aquatic Warbler. But I hadn't had my daily 'lifer'. So this had to be it. Andrew *had* seen an Aquatic, so he scampered off to telephone David Hunt, just in case he was free to come over from St Mary's. I was left to 'keep an eye' on the bird and with luck, identify it properly. Normally, I favour the 'wait-and-have-patience' approach to skulky birds but, after a while, I decided I could see no reason why this one should ever bother to poke its head out of the reeds, where it was presumably totally at home. I resolved to go in after it. I wasn't wearing wellies, so off came the shoes and socks, I rolled up my trousers, and in I went. For half an hour I squelched around, and the bird kept hidden. Then presumably it got bored with the game. As I paused to sigh, I sensed a movement behind me. I turned to see a little bundle of black and yellow stripes staring at me from the top of a stem. It was another of those 'you'll know it when you see it' birds. The books say that Aquatic and juvenile Sedge Warblers are similar. Wrong. Sedge Warblers look like Sedge Warblers. Aquatics look more like a cross between a tiger and a humbug!

Even as I clinched this rarity, I saw another one: a bird-watcher. Andrew had returned and with him was another birder, the first one we'd seen for a week! The Aquatic Warbler was no doubt equally amazed, and shinned further up its stem to get a better look. I pointed at it, and gave a 'thumbs-up' sign to Andrew and the newcomer. Andrew raised a celebratory fist in acknowledgement. Then I heard him tell the other bloke, 'It's an Aquatic.' The other birder raised his bins, and presumably saw the bird, though it can hardly have been more than a speck since they were some way away, back on 'dry land'. I heard Andrew ask, 'Is it new for you?' 'Yes,' the birder replied. Then he walked away. I couldn't believe it. A 'tick' maybe, but an Aquatic Warbler, hardly! The bird was clearly insulted. It shook its head in disgust, ceased posing, and dived back into the reeds.

Later in the day it had a more appreciative audience. David Hunt *had* been able to escape from the luminous anoraks for the afternoon, and, after we'd all enjoyed a largely liquid lunch at the island hostelry, we spent the afternoon by the pool, admiring the warbler from all possible angles. Andrew expressed his elation in a bizarre burst of athletic exuberance: he stood on his hands, did a couple of cartwheels, and fell in the mud, giggling hysterically. Not wise after a couple of pints of brown ale, but I knew what he meant.

DAY NINE

The last day. We started up at the Golf Course, where the Buff-breasted flock had increased to three. Then we joined David at Content Farm: not a bad name for the occasion, although maybe 'Deliriously Happy Farm' might have more accurately matched our mood. I'm not sure that the 'good bit' of Content really exists these days. The farm is still there, but I think access is restricted, and in any case the little marsh surrounded by willow trees has been largely filled in. This is a pity. It was one of those hidden hot spots that always felt like it was going to produce 'the big one'. That day, we thought we might have found it.

When we arrived, David was in a state somewhere between excitement and puzzlement. He told us there were several warblers in the willows. He'd seen Wood, Sedge, Reed, and Garden Warblers, and two Icterines. Also 'one other', which he couldn't identify. When a bird-watcher as experienced as David sees a 'mystery bird', it is almost as good as guaranteeing an extreme rarity. However, though David had seen the warbler several times, and put together a description, he still couldn't put a name to it. When he told us what it looked like, it sounded like a caricature of the original 'little brown job': 'Dull brown above, whitish below, whitish eyestripe, dull brown legs.' That sort of description could fit several species, but, as all bird-watchers appreciate, it is the 'jizz' of the thing that narrows it down. Which was the problem with this bird; it just wouldn't give any decent views.

Unfortunately, having pointed us at the willows, David had to go off and lead a party. I suppose he could have brought his clients to see the mystery bird, but he no doubt decided – quite correctly, I'm sure – that it would be exactly the sort of abstruse and tedious experience that might put them off birding for life! So Andrew and I were left to try and sort it out. We must have sat there for hours. We saw nothing. Until suddenly, up on to a tangle of dead twigs, hopped what had to be 'David's bird'. The description tallied. Yes, it was sort of 'dull brown and whitish'. But what about the all important 'jizz'? Well, frankly, it didn't have any! It had obviously just been bathing. It was soaked, its feathers were all ruffled up, and it had no more shape to it than a wet tissue. It looked more like a lavatory brush than a warbler. At least we thought it might have the grace to stay there and dry out and reveal its true contours. But no. As mysteriously as it had appeared, it vanished again. This time for ever.

To this day, I really don't know what it was. We tried a 'process of elimination' approach which took us through everything from Dusky Warbler to soaking Sedge Warbler, but none of them really fitted. The most disquieting theory grew out of the fact that, about two weeks later, a controversial warbler was found at Porthellick, which started out as an 'aberrant Sedge Warbler' and ended up – in a net – as a definite Paddyfield Warbler. Could our Content mystery have been an early sighting of that? Personally, I don't think so, but maybe that's only because I know I couldn't count it! In fact, I reckon the most likely explanation is that it was a Cetti's Warbler. Not, of course, a very rare bird, though at the time it would have been a first for Scilly. So why didn't three perfectly competent bird-watchers recognize it? Mmm. I dunno. Maybe it *wasn't* a Cetti's. It *was* good fun though. And so were the trio of Serins that were twittering in the weedy field alongside the warbler willows. 'Lifer' number eight. Nine days, eight 'lifers'. But what about that extra 'value'? Well....

The days were full of birds. The nights were full of music and romance. There was a lot of music on St Mary's in those days. The Mermaid pub was not only the 'official' place for visiting birders to meet up each evening – all four of us! – but it was also the venue for the weekly folk club upstairs, and rather more raucous 'jam sessions' downstairs. These featured, amongst others, a virtuoso washboard player who went, as I recall, by the nickname of 'Washboard'. Can't argue with that. Also starring was a rather mellifluous trombone player by the name of David Hunt. David had, in fact, in a 'previous life', been a professional musician, having played alongside various legendary figures of the British traditional jazz scene, as well as in blues bands that had included various eventual Rolling Stones. I'm not sure that from Mick Jagger to 'Washboard' was an upward career move, but David certainly seemed to enjoy himself. So did we all.

In addition to the music at the Mermaid, there was also a very lively weekly dance held up at the airport. The personnel of the band would vary from week to week, but the nucleus of it involved David's trombone, the excellent guitar playing of an American musician who was 'hanging out' in the islands, and the drumming of one of the local boatmen, who played the biggest drum kit you ever saw in your life. Apparently he'd 'rescued' it from a ship that had gone aground on the notorious Cornish coast, and which just happened to be carrying a consignment of musical instruments. The drum kit still had a few seaweed stains on it, and was held together with string – tied, I presume, in authentic nautical knots – but it certainly looked impressive. It also sounded incredibly loud, as I discovered when I was allowed to 'sit in' for a few numbers. Well I say, 'allowed'. In fact, drummers are notoriously possessive about allowing anyone else to play their kits, and the boatman was particularly reluctant to relinquish his seat to me. I think David probably had to threaten not to use his boat for his holiday cruises before he'd let me have a go. I don't know what he was so worried about. I reckoned any kit that could survive a couple of weeks under the sea could put up with me tapping it for ten minutes. Nevertheless, all the time I was playing, he just stood close by and glared at me. When he took over again, he hit the drums so hard it was almost as if he was beating the kit for being unfaithful! Was it Duke Ellington who wrote a piece called 'A drum is woman'? Quite so, not to be clobbered, but caressed.

Which brings me to romance. As well as the itinerant musicians on the islands, there was also a temporary influx of young people, who worked at the various hotels or restaurants. These included quite a lot of girls who, by September – the end of the holiday period – were bronzed, beautiful, full of the energy that comes from breathing in that invigorating sea air, and were looking for one last experience to make their season truly memorable. So was I. Fortunately, one of the girls found me. And vice versa. Andrew very considerately moved out of our hotel room and spent the night in a disused air-raid shelter, so that she and I could share a night of … well, I wouldn't call it 'passion'. More 'cuddly fun'. I'm not absolutely sure I remember her name, but two things I do remember: she had masses of soft curly hair, and she was lovely and warm. It wasn't love, but it was ever so nice.

So that was it. Booze, blues, birds, scenery and sex. Scilly in the Seventies. As a crusty old Prime Minister used to keep telling us: 'We never had it so good!'

3
Goodbye Dave
India

PAINTED STORKS

SHAPES of...

INDIA

WHITE BACKED VULTURES

WIRE TAILED SWALLOW

INDIAN DARTER

male PINE BUNTING

('Twitched' after Dave's "ashes" ceremony on St MARY'S ... I'm sure he would have approved! Oddly enough last one I saw was ... in INDIA.

I shall never forget that phone call.

'Hello, Bill … Bad news, I'm afraid. David has been killed by a tiger in India.' I put the phone down and told my wife, Laura. We held each other and cried.

The call had come from David Hunt's wife, Marianne. After a while, I called her back, but before that, a part of my life flashed before my eyes. They say that's what happens when you face your own death. Sometimes it also happens when you lose a friend. I suppose it's your brain trying to deny what's happened, as if it's saying the memories are still alive, so the person must be too.

I'd first met David when I had gone on my first trip to Scilly, some time at the end of the sixties, or maybe in the very early seventies. At the time I was appearing quite a lot on the television and, whilst I was enjoying the success, I wasn't always so good at coping with the attention that 'fame' brings with it. I tended to regard autograph hunters as an intrusion rather than a compliment and, if holidaymakers asked me to pose for a photograph with the children, I was just as likely to snarl as smile. My only excuse was that I suffered from a very real kind of claustrophobia. My abrasiveness may have lost me some friends, but it also gained me one. I think David had heard that I was staying on St Mary's and actually sought me out. I recall he tapped me on the shoulder as I was hurrying down the High Street on my first morning. I probably flinched or grimaced, but he firmly introduced himself: 'I'm David Hunt. You're Bill Oddie, aren't you?'

I am absolutely sure that David's motive had nothing at

all to do with 'chatting up' a supposed 'TV personality'. Quite the opposite, in fact. As it happened, the 'star' in Scilly was David himself. Certainly to the extent that he was constantly bring grilled by visitors for information, or being held responsible by the islanders if bird-watchers misbehaved by trespassing or trampling through crops. Moreover, David had been a successful jazz musician, and had toured all round Europe with some quite big names. The result was that he was well used to the kind of claustrophobic attention that I was susceptible to. What's more, he could be pretty abrasive himself! In short, I instantly knew that David 'understood'. We had a lot in common. We became very close friends.

It was a friendship that went well beyond birds. If ever he happened to be passing through London, he stayed at my house. He was instantly liked by my first wife Jean, by my daughters Kate and Bonnie, and particularly by Laura. It wasn't that he was 'jolly Uncle Dave' – by no means. In fact, he was just as likely to turn up, have a grumble about something, gobble up an evening meal, and fall asleep in front of the telly. But if he *did* chat or take an interest, you knew that it was entirely genuine. What's more, he always 'spoke his mind', as they say. It was this 'honesty' that made him perhaps, at first, a little daunting – 'cheeky', Kate called it! – but, ultimately, it also made him easy to get on with. He simply made himself at home and – even if he only called in once or twice a year – he became one of the family.

As it turned out, homes and families became something of a moot point with both of us. During the seventies, my life was going through a rather protracted 'reorganization' – euphemism for separation and divorce – whilst, back on Scilly, David had some difficult times to cope with. I always felt his morale was sort of symbolized by his living conditions. When he first invited me up to supper on St

Mary's, I found myself scrunched up in a tiny kitchen at one end of what looked like an old Scout hut. It was hardly bigger than a glorified garden shed, but a series of chipboard partitions created separate – if tiny – territories for David and Marianne, his two large sons, and a couple of rampant ferrets! After-dinner conversation wasn't easy, as we had to compete with the boys' various musical activities, which ranged from playing rock records – very loudly – or trumpet or electric guitar – even louder. I'll be honest, when it came to dealing with my social claustrophobia, dinner at David's was excellent aversion therapy. After an evening at the hut, I welcomed the holiday crowds in St Mary's High Street as the very definition of 'getting away from it all'. In truth, of course, going birding was the real escape, and I'm sure that's how David regarded it himself. Inevitably, the situation put a strain on his marriage, which, in turn, made him feel guilty. As we pottered round together searching for birds, we often found ourselves discussing 'life and relationships'.

Happily – for everyone involved – by the start of the eighties things had improved considerably. I'd found Laura. David and Marianne had moved to a spacious modern apartment on the edge of St Mary's. Moreover, David had come to terms with the ever escalating 'Scilly Season'. In the early days, I know he'd found the annual invasion of twitchers a trying test of his temper (which was fairly short!) Unfortunately, there were not infrequent instances of birding delinquency: gates left open, dry-stone walls knocked down, bulb-fields flattened. This was – understandably – much resented by the farmers who lived and worked on Scilly, and relationships became so bad that 'Bird-watchers Keep Out' notices became distressingly common. The local people tended to blame David. As far as they were concerned, he was the 'Bird Man' and was

responsible for 'inviting' the twitchers, and for controlling
them. He couldn't win with anyone. He'd find himself
having rows both with local farmers and with the birders.
It got so bad that he would always try to arrange a lecture
tour in October so he could get off the islands. However,
in 1981, the Porthcressa Restaurant – which was beneath
David's new apartment – became the venue for evening
get-togethers, where visiting birders would call a daily log,
exchange news, show slides, and so on. David realized that
the answer to birder/islander relations was organization,
not confrontation. The bird-watchers' 'Code of Conduct'
was formulated, publicized and generally adhered to,
communications were improved, and, most importantly,
the islanders began to appreciate that twitchers represen-
ted income rather than irritation. Probably both sides also
began to discover that most of them were pretty nice
people, too! I've always felt that many of the earlier
problems were caused by unfamiliarity. The islanders felt
literally invaded by an almost paramilitary army. A
phalanx of birders do tend to dress in khaki and brandish
'weapons' that look disturbingly like mortars! But, some
time in the early eighties, they decided to call a truce and
get together. It was a bit like that song from *Oklahoma!*:
'The Farmers and the Birders Should be Friends'.

As it happens, it was a dance that perhaps best
symbolized the new bonhomie of the Scilly Season: the
Bird-watcher's Ball, to which everyone had to come
dressed as their favourite bird. David went as a
Yellow-bellied Sapsucker, a species he'd added to the
British list in 1975.

The fact is, I could write a book about the 'life and times
of David Hunt', but there is no need. He did it himself, and
it is called *Confessions of a Scilly Birdman*, though I fear it
may now be out of print (which is a pity, 'cos it's a jolly
good read). Early in 1985, David plonked the manuscript

on my kitchen table. He was passing through London on his way to India. He'd begun working for Cygnus Wildlife Holidays, and had led tours to the Pyrenees and West Africa. But India was his favourite, and this was to be his fifth visit. On the morning he left for the airport, I remember asking him if he'd ever seen a tiger. He replied that no, he'd never had a decent view, and that he'd really love to get some photographs of one. Maybe this time he'd be lucky. So off he went, leaving me to read his life story, and to write a foreword for it. This is part of what I wrote:

I'm assuming that if you are reading this, you are a bird-watcher. There can't be many bird-watchers who haven't heard of the Isles of Scilly; and there's probably not a lot who haven't been there at one time or another. At the very least, you must have browsed through the small ads at the back of *Birds* magazine or *British Birds*. In which case, you'll certainly know the name of David Hunt. Maybe you've just seen his little advert in its nice square box; 'Enjoy the Holiday of a Lifetime, with the Man on the Spot' (David Hunt). Or maybe you've even spotted the man himself. Maybe you've even spoken to him, though perhaps you didn't realize who he was at the time. I didn't know who he was when I first met him, and, if I hadn't seen him on and off for the last fifteen years, I don't think I'd recognize him if I met him again today. His appearance has changed quite a bit. Back in the 60s (or was it early 70s?) he resembled a rather morose overweight Beatle (a 'She Loves You, Yeah Yeah Yeah' Beatle – not an insect). Nowadays, he's slimmer, better groomed, altogether more dashing, I think, more confident and – dare I say it? – happier. In fact, he even seems younger. How he's come to arrive at this enviable condition is told in this book.

I wrote that a few days before I got the phone call. 'Killed by a tiger.' It sounded so bizarre that part of me had trouble taking it seriously. A heart-attack, a car crash, these are circumstances that are chillingly and unambiguously 'real'. But man-eating tigers belong in adventure stories or Tarzan movies. I honestly think my initial reaction was a nervous disbelieving laugh. It couldn't be true. But I knew it was. And I cried. Eventually, I rang Marianne back. She told me as much as she knew about the circumstances. She also said that she'd phoned me immediately because she was pretty certain that the press would get on to me, and she didn't want me to hear what had happened from a journalist. She was right. During the next hour I was called by several newspapers. They all wanted me to confirm one fact:

'David was a close friend of Prince Charles, wasn't he?'

I told them, 'No, he wasn't.'

'But he did know him, didn't he?' they insisted.

Again I told them, 'No. He didn't "know" him.'

I recalled that the Prince *had* once paid a visit to the islands, and it was possible that David had been briefly introduced as the 'local naturalist', but that was about it. He was certainly *not* a close friend. The journalists thanked me, and wrote their headlines. They were all the same:

'Close Friend of Charles Killed in India'.

Never let the facts get in the way of a good story.

With the agreement of Marianne and David's sons, the publishers decided to go ahead with the publication of *Confessions of a Scilly Birdman*. Hardly a month after writing the foreword, I found myself writing a postscript. Again, I quote:

'You're far too young to have written your autobiography.' So spoke a friend early in 1985. A few weeks later

David Hunt died. The circumstances were almost unbelievable. He was leading a party of bird-watchers through the Corbett National Park in northern India. He spotted a rare owl and, warning the rest of the party to wait and stick together, he set off in pursuit of the bird. He followed it out of sight over a ridge. There, he was attacked by a tiger and killed....

... Not much that David did in life could be described as 'ordinary', and so it was to the end. Considering the imminent publication of this book I have a feeling his own wry comment would have been: 'anything for publicity!' ...

... When he died, David was 51. He *was* far too young. He was unique, talented, and quite irreplaceable. I, and many others, miss him very much indeed. Scilly will never be the same again.

Scilly never *was* the same again. I continued to visit the islands, but everywhere I went would revive vivid memories of being in those places with David. I remembered the birds we shared and the exact circumstances. I sat on the rocks overlooking the main valley on Bryher and I could 'see' David leading his little crocodile of luminous anoraks along the road below me. I'd called out: 'Guess what I've seen!' 'Great Spotted Cuckoo', he'd shouted back. He'd seen it too. His clients had been more interested in the Stonechats! We grinned at each other. Whenever I walked under the pine trees by the Tresco Great Pool I heard the 'tchick' of the 1973 Myrtle Warbler. 'We'll pick it up by its call', I'd assured David. He'd seemed sceptical – and I was eternally grateful to the bird for proving me right! On the far side of St Martin's we'd enjoyed one of those lovely 'good timing' moments you get just now and then. 'Looks like a good place for a Tawny Pipit,' I'd suggested. 'Like that one there!' added David, as the bird instantly trotted out of the grass. I relived the delights of September 1974: the shark-fishing trip, the St Agnes Aquatic, the Content Farm mystery warbler. They were happy memories, and I felt comforted that David was still 'very much alive'. Inevitably, though, I also felt distressed and dismayed that he wasn't. I couldn't help reconstructing in my mind what must have happened in India. I'd spoken to someone who'd actually been on the trip and he had confirmed the basis of the story.

The only bit I'd got wrong in my postscript was the status of the owl. It hadn't been a rare one, it had been a Spotted Owlet, which is a pretty common bird in India. David, his co-leader, and their party, had been returning on foot to the accommodation block at Corbett National Park when the bird had flown across the path. David had announced that he was going to stay and try to photograph it. He suggested that the others left him there, and they had carried on walking back to base. It seems that the owl must have flown ahead of David into the forest. He had followed it. In a clearing, he had disturbed what was probably a female tiger close to her cubs. No doubt feeling it needed to protect its young, it had attacked and killed him. The co-leader was still not a long way down the path, and had even heard a yell, followed by an ominous silence. He feared what had happened. David's body was recovered later that day – or possibly the next morning – fortunately largely undisfigured. This much I had even 'seen for myself' in a short scene from a television documentary about tigers. It was a mercifully distant image, but it truly haunted me. At least, as the commentary confirmed, he must have died instantly. He was cremated in Delhi, and his ashes flown back to England. It all just seemed like a terrible tragic accident, a million-to-one chance.

Nevertheless, it put me off India for years. I had, in fact, been on a wonderful trip there in 1979 and had, at the time, vowed to go back as soon as possible. And yet, though I was offered several chances to return, I always turned them down. I resorted to a variety of 'excuses'. I was 'too busy'; 'I didn't want to leave Laura and our new daughter Rosie'; 'I was scared by reports of political unrest and rioting', and so on. Eventually, though, I had to admit to myself that what *really* scared me was what had happened to David. It wasn't that I thought it could possibly happen to me, it was that I really didn't want to confront the scene of the incident. Then, in 1993, I received another invitation to go to India. It was for three weeks' filming, and included an itinerary which would involve visiting Corbett National Park itself. It was to be in late February, the same month as David's fateful visit. Moreover, I was now fifty-one myself. I could almost hear David's voice telling me I'd be a bloody fool if I chickened out.

The documentary I was to be involved in was a pretty quirky concept. It involved cycling up the Ganges on a three-seater bicycle, the other two saddles occupied by a young environmentalist film-maker and an Australian didgeridoo player! The environmentalist would be examining pollution along the Holy River, the Australian would be searching for his 'spiritual roots', and I would be bird-watching. It was quite an eventful journey, but that's another story (and a fascinating one, though to date we have had trouble convincing television companies). I did also, of course, have an additional theme that I intended to investigate. How would I feel when I retraced David's last footsteps? And would I discover any more information about what had happened?

We started in Calcutta, where I talked to Belinda Wright. She had been working with tigers for many years, studying

and filming them. She told me that she had met David at
the fabulous Bharatpur bird sanctuary, back in February
1985. She had reason to remember the evening very
clearly. Over supper, David's clients had been asking her
all sorts of questions about India's wildlife, and about
tigers in particular. Belinda is an articulate, intelligent,
extremely knowledgeable, and disarmingly modest
woman. There is no way that she would sensationalize the
nature of her work. Nevertheless, it seems that David was
sceptical when she stressed the dangers involved. After the
rest of the party had retired, he and Belinda continued
talking. She told me that the conversation became
increasingly acrimonious. It seemed that David was, in
effect, accusing Belinda of exaggerating the risks of
walking and working in tiger country and, in doing so,
was implying that she was 'showing off', presumably to
impress David and his clients. Belinda became, understandably – and I think totally justifiably – angry about this.
Why David was taking this stance I can only conjecture.
Maybe he had 'promised' his party that they stood a good
chance of seeing tigers at Corbett, and had assured them
that walking in the park would be perfectly safe. Maybe he
was concerned that Belinda's caution might have
frightened them. Maybe he was so set on seeing and
photographing a tiger himself that he really 'didn't want to
know' about any dangers. Or maybe he really did think
that the odds against an attack were so high that it simply
wasn't worth bothering about. In any event, it seems that
he insisted he was right. To quote Belinda's own word –
used, I might add, with no malice at all – she said that she
found his attitude ultimately rather 'objectionable'. They
bade each other good night, with her wishing him a good
trip, but ending with a final warning:

'When you are in tiger country, I suggest you be very
careful indeed.'

Two days later he was killed.

Two weeks after talking to Belinda, I found myself approaching Corbett National Park. Heaven knows it didn't feel like the gateway to danger. The approach road passed through countryside that reminded me of a particularly gentle part of agricultural France – lush cornfields, cows, children playing outside the occasional sleepy farmhouse. I was aware that this wasn't the main park, as we were driving along by a tall wire fence, but, even when we arrived at the actual entrance, it looked more like the reception area of a children's zoo than anything to be scared about. There was a large sign saying 'Project Tiger' above the gate, and I noticed that the guard had a rifle propped against his chair, but there was also a small reception kiosk selling sweets and soft drinks, and a dozy little deer came snuffling up to the window of our vehicle to be patted and fed. If I'd been dropped blindfold on a parachute, I would have thought I'd landed at the entrance to Windsor Safari Park.

The only thing quintessentially Indian about it was the 'pratting' before we were eventually allowed in. The producer of our film had made the booking months ago, and it had been confirmed by phone as soon as we arrived in the country. Nevertheless, we'd called in at the local town, where the Project Tiger headquarters were situated, just to make sure everything was in order. There, we'd been told that they'd never heard of us! In India, one soon learns that such a totally negative response is merely there to be questioned. In fact, the producer soon proved that they *had* heard of us, by finding our names in the booking ledger – they had all been crossed out! It was then explained that Lady Somebody from Delhi had fancied a weekend at Corbett with her entourage, so they'd given her our rooms. Oh, was *that* all! You don't let little things like that put you off in India, either. So we'd driven to the official 'check-in' office in the village closest to the park. They *had* heard of us there, and they even confirmed that our rooms had been reserved. Now that we were at the actual entrance lodge, they *hadn't* heard of us again! Fortunately, the guard didn't feel like an argument that day, and he could see that we were a real film crew, with real cameras, and real money to pay for our permits ... so he let us in.

At the accommodation centre at Dakhala, in the middle of the park, we discovered the true situation about our booking. Yes, they *had* heard of us, yes, our bookings *had* been cancelled to make room for Lady Somebody, but yes, they *had* still got room for us. As it happens, it turned out to be *a* room, rather than the several we needed for a party of eight, but, fortunately, it was warm and dry enough for 'the young people' in the crew to sleep on the roof. I, being older and grumpier, was allowed to have a roof over my head. I also had a ceiling, which contained a· cold-water pipe that leaked all over my bed. Never mind. I was there. This is where David and his party would have stayed. I went outside, glared at Lady Somebody, who was being fawned over and photographed in front of 'our' rooms, walked to the terrace, and gazed out over Corbett National Park.

So this was tiger country. It looked gorgeous. Immediately below the terrace was a sort of green cliff covered in bushes which were, in turn, covered in parakeets. Beneath the cliff ran a shallow river, clean and pebbly, looking more as though it belonged in the Welsh valleys than in India. The only thing not Welsh about it was a large elephant sitting on its back legs and being scrubbed down by its mahout. Beyond the river was a wide flat plain, maybe a mile across, much of it as open as a cricket pitch, but with other areas covered in taller vegetation. I think they call it elephant grass, which is fair enough because, when I scanned with my binoculars, I realized there were indeed several genuinely wild Indian elephants grazing in it. Beyond the plain, the forest rose gently towards the horizon across several ridges, each one getting higher till they reached the sky. I had a strange feeling that I recognized that part of the view. Had I seen it on the television? In a documentary about tigers?

The 'lodge' at Dakhala is in an enclosure surrounded by a clearly marked boundary. It is hardly a safe compound, as the fence – where it exists at all – is no more than a chain about two foot off the ground. There are two or three unsurfaced roads leading to and from the area. The temptation to go wandering is almost irresistible. Within twenty minutes, I had succumbed to it. Within twenty yards, I was stopped in my tracks. Yellow and black stripes. No, not the real thing. A brick sign – shaped I thought rather too like a gravestone – with a bold outline of a tiger on it. The jungle equivalent of a 'Beware – Cattle Crossing' sign? It was clearly more than that. 'No Entry', in fact. Nevertheless, the land beyond was so open that there was no way a kitten could have hidden in it, let alone a tiger. Besides, I wanted to see what was on the other side of the sign. I scurried past and looked back. There was a large black paw print painted on it, and something written in 'Indian' script. Perhaps that was for any tigers who wandered along the road to read. Presumably it said 'Please don't eat the tourists'. Even as I entertained such whimsical thoughts, I realized that I was, in fact, feeling very nervous. There was no way I could have taken another step down the track and, even if I could have done, I wouldn't have been allowed to. 'Oi!' came a loud voice. It was probably said in the local dialect, but 'Oi!' is the same in any language. Whether it is a farmer chasing a twitcher off his land, or the head ranger warning you about tigers, 'Oi!' means 'Get out of there! Now!'

So I did. I took one step back behind the tiger sign and began to talk to the man who'd shouted 'Oi!' He told me that visitors were not allowed out of the compound on foot. Obviously things had been different eight years ago. I had to ask.

'Was this after the Englishman was killed?'

'David Hunt? Yes.'

Again, I had to ask him.

'Were you working here then?'

'Yes,' he replied. 'It was very unwise of him,' he continued, 'when he *knew* there was a tiger nearby.'

I was taken aback.

'When he knew? What do you mean?'

He told me the story. When he'd finished, I asked him: 'Where exactly did it happen?'

He pointed across the valley, to where the forest began to climb.

'Across there, just over the first ridge.'

That evening, we took an elephant ride in search of tigers. That's how they do it nowadays. We set out like a circus parade – four elephants, with four people on each. Plus the mahout, who sits astride the animal's head and occasional whacks it with a vicious-looking spiky metal thing. Apparently this feels like no more than a tickle to an elephant. Mind you, the mahout told us that, not the elephant. After leaving the compound, each elephant takes its own course, guided by its mahout. Ours slowly descended a steep path down the green cliff, waded through the river, and then ambled around the valley for an hour or two. Down in the plain, you realize just how high the elephant grass is. Elephants can actually hide in some of it. A couple of hundred tigers could hold a barn dance down there and you wouldn't notice them! You might hear them; in fact, we *thought* we did hear a distant roar. But it might have been a flatulent elephant, or a

Land-Rover revving up. No one on any of the elephants saw a tiger on that ride; nor on any of the other rides during the long weekend that we were at Corbett. We hadn't even seen any tracks, or 'pug-marks', as the paw prints are called. Unlike David.

Next day, I got our driver to take me over to the other side of the valley. There was an observation tower there, from the top of which you could scan the terrain or the canopy, and try and spot animals and birds. In truth, there wasn't very much to see that day. It was all very, very quiet, the only sound the gentle swishing of the breeze in the elephant grass. But just because we couldn't see anything didn't mean there wasn't something out there. It took me back to one of the only other times I'd knowingly been in 'tiger country'. That was in Thailand in 1980. I was on a birding trip with three friends and again we were staying inside a national park. We knew there were tigers in the area because we'd seen one in a cage; apparently, it had been killing the local farmer's cattle. They had managed to capture it alive, and presumably it was now being carted off to Bangkok zoo, or – knowing Thailand's unfortunate skin trade – it might well have ended up as a rug. We had been assured that tigers were very rare in the park (I bet they were!) and that we had nothing to fear. Nevertheless, I recall walking to a similar tower hide one evening, along a track cut between tall grass, and being aware that a tiger could have been sitting inches away from us and we really would never have seen it.

The tiger's stripes are brilliant camouflage and, especially if it crouches down, it can hide in very sparse cover. I knew this because I had almost obsessively watched every television programme about tigers over the years. As it happens, one of the programmes had been largely filmed at a place I had visited on my only other trip to India, back in 1979. Ranthanbore was, even then, a declared tiger reserve, but on our visit the nearest we had got to encountering a tiger was being shown a couple of old pug-marks by a park ranger. They had been conveniently close to the track, and we'd only had to lean out of the Land-Rover to see them. I couldn't help wondering if the ranger had made them himself for the tourists. At Ranthanbore we had wandered around on foot every day bird-watching, and never even thought about tigers. I felt a distinct shudder when I eventually saw the film on television, for it featured tigers patrolling the very same jungle trails we had walked along. Was it that tigers had got much bolder at Ranthanbore? Or had we been in much greater danger than we realized? I also wondered whether we would have walked along those trails had we *known* there really were tigers in the area. That evening at Corbett, I thought about what I'd just been told: 'David knew'. And I shuddered again.

I scanned the scene below the tower. I saw no animals, but I *did* recognize the view. We'd arrived at the hide by driving along a trail through the forest. Now, when I looked back, I could see that it had emerged into a more open area, where the hide was sited. Close to the track the bushes were low and the trees sparse; then the forest began to thicken as the land rose to the top of a small ridge. Beyond the ridge was the real jungle. This was the place. As if compelled, I climbed down the stairs from the tower, and walked just a few yards back along the track. I reconstructed in my mind the story that the ranger had told me back at the compound.

David, his co-leader, and his party had been walking on foot along this trail. But there had been one more person with them, an Indian guide who apparently always accompanied visiting groups. Suddenly, the guide had stopped and pointed to the ground in front of them. He had whispered the word that, to be truthful, all visitors to

Corbett want to hear: 'Tiger!' There were pug-marks on the path. Not fake ones. Definitely real.

'A tiger has walked across this path,' the guide told them.

'How long ago?' asked David.

'Recently,' replied the guide.

'How recently?' David persisted. 'Yesterday? Today?'

'Very recently,' the guide answered. 'A tiger has walked across this path very recently. Today.'

The group carried on down the trail, no doubt with hearts beating faster and pulses racing. They hadn't gone far when a Spotted Owlet flew across and landed in a nearby tree.

'Look,' said David, pointing out the bird to his party. They watched it. The owl showed no inclination to move, so David got out his camera and telephoto lens.

'I'm going to try and get some decent photos of it,' he announced. 'You all go on to the lodge. I'll be back soon.' The rest of the party carried on down the track. Whether the guide warned David, I don't know. And if he did, did David dismiss his caution as 'scaremongering', just as he had Belinda's?

In any event, we know what happened next. The owl flew on over the ridge. David followed. He disturbed the tiger. It killed him.

Terrible luck. Or terrible judgement? Or was it a calculated risk?

David *knew* there had been a tiger in the area not too long ago. He must also have known it might still be close by, and yet he went in pursuit of a Spotted Owlet. A Spotted Owlet is not a rare bird in India; they are common and trusting. It is not hard to get a decent picture of a Spotted Owlet. It is not worth risking your life for.

It is not so easy to get a photograph of a tiger.

I believe that David stayed behind precisely *because* he'd

been told there might be a tiger close by. I believe he was intent on getting some decent photographs of it. He got them.

When David's body was recovered, so was his camera. Later on, the slides were developed, and in April 1985 Marianne showed them to me. The first one is a nice close-up of a Spotted Owlet sitting on a branch. David must have been crouched under the tree, using a 300-millimetre lens. Then he must have heard a noise behind him, or maybe just sensed that he was not alone. Keeping crouched, he turned and saw a tiger pacing to and fro at the edge of the clearing. The next slide is of the tiger. It is some way away, walking to the right. On the next picture it is walking to the left. In the next one, it is facing the camera. In the next, it has begun to move forward, still looking straight at the lens. The next is closer. Then closer. And closer still. The final picture is a frame-filling shot of the tiger's head, eyes blazing and teeth exposed in a snarl. If David had just kept shooting on his motor-drive, the whole thing must have happened in barely ten seconds. Crouched behind a camera, looking through the viewfinder and especially when using a telephoto lens, you don't realize how close your subject has got. Neither, at the time, do you care. All you are focusing on is the picture. Press cameramen in war situations call it 'camera blindness'. It has proved fatal before.

It was a beautiful spring evening when a small gathering assembled on the top of Penninis Head, on St Mary's, Scilly, to scatter David's ashes to the winds that had brought him so much pleasure in the form of migrant birds. I hadn't intended to make a 'speech', but when the time came I couldn't stop myself. I don't suppose much of it was terribly coherent, but I do recall suddenly observing that, to any distant bird-watcher, the little crowd, all gathered intently at one spot, must have looked like a bunch of twitchers concentrating on a rarity. I half expected a frantic birder to appear over the horizon, come panting up to us, and ask: 'What have you got?'

I'm sure David would have laughed. He would probably also have called him a bloody fool.

I suppose that maybe he took some things too seriously, and others not seriously enough.

4
If You Ever Go Across the Sea to ...
Ireland

WILSON'S PETREL
"performing"....
(for some..).

Flap & Glide.
- uniform underwing
- protruding feet

white
under wing
Stormy
(for comparison)

more or less
from
'field sketches'
- well, 'sea sketches'..
which is why they're not very sure!

IRELAND
...VARIOUS AUTUMNS...

SEMI PALMATED SANDPIPER x1

BUFF BREASTED
SANDPIPER
x 2

BAIRD'S
SANDPIPER x 3

Foot about lifesize
(the bird isn't...but
it was).

" THE TACUMSHIN
COLLECTION "

(the numbers are birds present
of each species NOT the scale!).

PECTORAL
SANDPIPER
x 4

WILSON'S x 2
PHALAROPE

If you *do* ever go across the sea to Ireland, then you'll discover that not all the cliché images of the Emerald Isle are entirely accurate. That's the conclusion I've come to, anyway. And I've been to Ireland many times. Well, I've been to the South (the Republic; Eire) many times. As it happens, even as I write, I've just set up my very first visit to the North (Ulster), having been asked to open Ireland's first Bird Fair at Strangford Lough later in spring. I'm looking forward to it very much.

Meanwhile, back to the South. So what are these cliché images? Well, you know what I mean. The stuff you see in the movies, or on postcards in the airport souvenir shop: women in headscarves carrying baskets of peat, old fellas in black suits with flat caps and wooden pipes, traffic-free lanes full of sheep and donkeys, and villages with cobbled streets and lopsided pubs full of ruddy-faced locals drinking Guinness, speaking Gaelic, and dancing Irish reels or singing about leprechauns. Well, no doubt you can find such things if you look for them, particularly if you nip into the local tourist office and ask what's on, or tag along with the nearest gaggle of American tourists seeking their roots. But if you're bird-watching, it's likely you'll get a different picture.

It often strikes me that birders don't have a normal 'take' on whatever country they happen to visit. Usually they are belting round in a (probably hired) car, following carefully researched instructions from site to site, ticking off 'target species', or trying to increase their trip list. Occasionally, we may stop for a few days at a place and get to know it better, but I fear we still often remain largely oblivious to the things that most normal visitors appreciate, like scenery, nice weather, food, accommodation, local attractions, and so on. All we usually really care about is – the birds. Moreover, we often visit these places outside the normal holiday season, which can also give a somewhat distorted – or at least different – view of a country.

Let me be more specific. Over the years, I'd been birding many many times in Ireland. All my visits had been either in midwinter or in late autumn. I had driven all over the place. The things I'd really appreciated were empty roads, unspoilt countryside, and the birds. As far as I was concerned, this was a definition of Utopia. Easy to drive from place to place, nobody to annoy you when you got there, and lots of birds to look at. That was Ireland. I wouldn't have a word said against it. It took an out of season non-bird-watching visit to demist slightly my rose-tinted spectacles.

This was a 'long weekend' in midsummer (early August) when I was supposed to be writing a 'travel' article for a newspaper. I suggested that my wife Laura should come along. She'd never been to Ireland. 'You'll love it,' I assured her. Well … she did, eventually. However, I sensed that her first impression was less than favourable, as we attempted to escape from the confusing maze of mini-motorways outside Shannon Airport. 'We'll be out in a minute,' I chuckled nervously, implying that secluded roads and green hills were just around the corner. In fact, what was around the corner was an even bigger motorway, with hundreds of heavy goods lorries thundering along past – not green hills – but miles of grey factories. It's called 'Shannon Initiative Zone', or something like that, which is a euphemism for … miles of factories. A sign of a burgeoning economy maybe, but not what I'd promised Laura. I apologized. 'But you've been here before. Surely you must have known it was like this?' she asked, rather accusingly, I thought. The truth was that I *had* been there before – many times – but I'd honestly never noticed how unsightly it all was. To a birder such as I, the motorway was merely a conveniently quick way of getting to the good bits – the quiet places. 'OK. So, any chance of going to those, then?' enquired Laura. 'That's *exactly* where we're going,' I assured her. 'What's more, we'll take the back route. Oh, I love these Irish roads. You can drive for miles without seeing another car.' So saying, I turned off the motorway, and into a traffic jam. The quiet roads weren't quiet at all. They were choked bumper-to-bumper with holidaymakers. As we crawled along, I felt guilty and claustrophobic. Not a sensation I associated with Ireland.

Of course – it suddenly struck me – whenever I'd been in the area before, I'd been going to bird spots. Where the tourists don't go. I suddenly became decisive: 'There's a seabird reserve not too far away, we'll go there,' I announced. There was a signpost. We followed it. So did everyone else. The Cliffs of Moher may indeed be a seabird colony, but they are also one of Ireland's greatest tourist attractions. There was a car park big enough to serve Wembley Stadium – though *not* the Cliffs of Moher, as it was overflowing – and a crowd that looked as if it belonged at a cross between an international Scout jamboree and an open-air rock concert. There were giggling gaggles of young folk in luminous anoraks from all over the world: Germany, Holland, America, Japan … just about every country, except Ireland. The only Irish people there were trying to persuade the foreign visitors to buy things. Irish things, but with sort of 'hippy' connections, like tie-dyed T-shirts with pictures of James Joyce on them, or portraits of Oscar Wilde in a cloud of opium. There were also lots of stalls selling joss-sticks and beads, as well as the more traditional fare of shamrocks and shillelaghs. And there was all sorts of Irish music emanating from tapes and buskers; everything from the traditional pipes and fiddles to U2, via the Pogues, Bob Geldof, Josef Locke, and the Nolan Sisters. In fact, it was quite an impressive reminder of what a musical race the Irish are. Though I couldn't help feeling it would have been more effective if everyone hadn't been singing at the same time. OK. Second moment of realization. On previous trips I'd not only been visiting remote bird spots, but also it had *not* been the first week of August.

I couldn't change the date, but I could change the venue. I suggested to Laura that we should go in search of some lunch. 'There must be a nice Irish country pub round here somewhere.'

Indeed there was, but not one that did lunch. We fancied something more than a Guinness and a packet of crisps, so we decided to go and check in to our hotel, which was in the nearby town. Even as we approached the outskirts, I somehow knew Laura wasn't going to be impressed by Irish architecture. Or maybe it's the town planning that is at fault: like there doesn't seem to be any! I'm not going to name the town we were approaching (it wouldn't be fair, 'cos it has got lots of good points, and its architecture is no worse or better than average), but, be honest, it really was a bit of a mess. (And still is, no doubt.) Again, to be fair, there are plenty of unprepossessing towns all over the world. I suppose it's just that the countryside in much of Ireland really is so stunning, that you desperately *want* the towns to be as attractive. But they're not.

There have been many hard times in Irish history, and village architecture must have suffered accordingly. These days things are much more prosperous but, ironically, part of the problem is that – how can I put this? – er ... wealth and good taste don't always seem to go together. On the other hand, the results can be quite entertaining, if you like modern bungalows with Doric columns at the front door, or six-foot golden eagles as your gateposts. Maybe it's all for the benefit of those root-seeking Americans. Maybe they feel more at home if Irish housing estates remind them of Dallas! And talking of the American influence in Ireland, please *don't* be disappointed if you pop into a bar of an evening to hear a local ceilidh band and find them playing old Jim Reeves numbers. Ireland has produced some wonderful musicians, but when it comes down to folk music in the true sense – i.e. what 'the people' like! – it's Country and Western.

In fact, by the end of our weekend, Laura was as captivated by the country as I always have been, and – I'm delighted to say – she keeps asking to go back. As if I need an excuse! As I said at the beginning of this chapter, not all the Irish clichés apply. The ones that are undeniable – and are truly to be treasured – are the delights of Irish hospitality, the scenery, and, of course, the birds!

My first birding trip over there was some time back in the early seventies. I had been browsing through old Irish Bird Reports, and I kept reading about places that seemed to attract more American waders than America. I was enthralled at the idea that these birds really did cross the Atlantic. I still am. I mean, OK, the west coast of Ireland may be the nearest bit of Europe to the United States (I'm not counting Iceland or Greenland, that's 'Father Christmas land', not Europe), but it's still a heck of a long way. Maybe the birds do get blown along by westerly gales, but I'm still impressed. I'd also be very grateful if they'd stick around long enough for me to see them. I'd like to think that the birds would be grateful, too. Surely it must be some consolation for the fact that you've pitched down in County Cork when you'd meant to fly to the West

Indies, if at least you know you're being admired and appreciated? I felt I had a duty to go and make them feel wanted. So, one September, I flew to Shannon, hired a car, and set out on my first 'Yankee wader' tour. I was not disappointed. At Akeagh Lough in County Kerry I saw my first Buff-breasted Sandpiper, and at Ballycotton, in Cork, I was able to enjoy an American Lesser Golden Plover, sitting on the beach writing a script for *Doctor in the House*. (I was writing the script, not the plover.)

My next quest was to try and see a real wild Snow Goose (as opposed to an 'escape') and a genuine Canada Goose (as opposed to anything in England). So I found myself in Wexford in the middle of winter. (The city of Wexford is, incidentally, the only Irish town I know that actually does have a cobbled street with nothing but higgledy-piggledy bars in it – though it is only *one* street.) Just outside the town are the Wexford Slobs. These are not local reprobates, but vast wetlands that just happen to be amongst the best places in the world for seeing wild geese. The experience is made all the more enjoyable because you can use your car as a mobile hide. You simply drive slowly along the farm tracks and the geese carry on feeding in the nearby fields, giving you lots of time to sort through them. Well, they do on a good day! If you're not so lucky, you can drive round and round for hours, wondering how on earth you can 'lose' a few thousand enormous birds that normally honk noisily and draw attention to themselves. On the day I went the birds were very co-operative (they usually are if you give them time). Amongst the huge flock of Greenland White-fronts, I picked out a 'blue phase' Snow Goose, a 'small' Canada Goose (but big enough to have 'made in Canada' stamped on it), and – as a bonus – what looked like a hybrid between the two. I often feel that hybrids are probably the result of captive birds getting bored and indulging in a little sexual experimentation (and who can blame them?), but I was sure that this one was proof that such shenanigans went on in the wild as well. Well, it must get awfully chilly up there in Arctic Canada. I guess you grab hold of anything that will warm you up.

So, that was two successful Irish missions completed, and in subsequent seasons there were more. And the only thing rarer than the birds was the bird-watchers. On all my early visits I hardly met any. When I did, it was a pleasure to have someone to chat to for while, unlike in England where, even back in the seventies, I was beginning to get put off by the inevitable crowds that gathered at any hot spots. I don't know whether it's because I'm unsociable, or because I don't like the 'competition', or because I'm sort of 'pioneering' by nature, but the fact is that I have always been perfectly happy birding on my own. However ... there's a difference between being alone, and being lonely. It was on one of my Irish jaunts that I decided I was exactly that. I'd gone over in March to see if I could tick off some more 'Yanks'. On the first day, I did see a Long-billed Dowitcher and get a distant glimpse of a Green-winged Teal at Ballycotton, but somehow the experience lacked something. Somebody to share it with, perhaps? Heavens, was I becoming sentimental in my middle age? As I set off on the long drive north to Kerry, I suddenly felt quite panicky. Could I really face three hours in the car listening to Terry Wogan soundalikes on the radio, or non-stop Country and Western music, or, worse still, talking to myself, or just thinking? Answer: NO. I turned round, drove back to Cork airport, and – although I'd hardly been in the country more than twenty-four hours – flew home. I resolved that the next time I visited Ireland, it would be with a birding chum.

Thus it was that, on 12 September 1980, Tony Marr and I boarded the car ferry from Fishguard (in Pembrokeshire, Wales) to Rosslare (in Wexford, Ireland).

It turned out to be one of the most enjoyable and successful trips I've ever been on. Even as we stood at the back of the boat watching the Welsh coastline disappear in our wake, we had one of those experiences bird-watchers dream about. We'd already 'got our eye in' on Manx Shearwaters. Then Tony picked out a Storm Petrel fluttering across our bows. Perhaps because it was a lone bird we studied it carefully, taking in the salient points. Then, give minutes later, as if programmed to appear for an instant comparison, along glided another petrel. I suppose that was what first set the alarm bells ringing in my head: the bird was *gliding*, not fluttering like a 'Stormy'. It was clearly something different, but what? Would it turn tail and disappear over the waves, as so many seabirds do? Or would it give us a fair chance to sort it out?

Well, you know birders talk about rare birds 'performing'? You may hear the expression if you ring up Birdline: 'The Pallas's Warbler was seen again this morning in Holkham Woods. It was performing well.' To me this always conjures up a picture of a bird with a straw hat and a cane doing a tap-dance and singing 'Hey, Look Me Over' (if only they did!). But what it really means is that it's sitting there or flitting around in full view, so that the twitchers can tick it off immediately, and be off to the next tick without having to hang around wasting time doing any proper bird-watching. Personally, I quite enjoy it if a rarity makes you work a bit before giving itself up (as long as it *does* give itself up eventually). However, when you've just spotted a mystery petrel at 200 yards from the back of a car ferry, you do rather hope it will 'perform' for you. We didn't need the straw hat and cane; all we asked for was a decent close view. Well, if we'd had the bird on remote control we couldn't have got a more co-operative 'performance'. It flapped and glided closer to the ship.

Then it took up a position about 50 yards away and flew parallel to us for some five minutes, allowing us to appreciate its dark underwing, protruding feet, and wrap-around white rump. All of which added up to an undeniable Wilson's Petrel – at the time, about the fourth British record! The alarm bells turned to peals of celebration as the bird waved us goodbye and veered off towards the horizon. What a start to a birding week.

We were still chuckling with elation as the boat slowed down to avoid crashing into Ireland. Our euphoria was tainted with a tiny tinge of guilt as we crossed over to the starboard side and discovered a couple more bird-watchers. Tony and I looked at each other. We looked at the other birders. They looked at us. They didn't look as happy as we did. So, were we going to tell them or not? You bet we were! Though we were, of course, sensitive enough to break it to them gently.

'Er ... have you been sea-watching from that side then?'

'Yes.'

'Anything?'

'Not a lot. Just a few "Stormies".'

This was our chance to be humble, before sticking the knife in.

'Oh we only had one "Stormy". We er ... we did have a Wilson's, though.'

I felt obliged to show them my field sketches to prove that we weren't stringing, but on reflection maybe it would have been kinder to let them think we were. Apparently, these birders were based at a nature reserve in Wales, and were in the habit of occasionally doing a round trip on the ferry in the hope of seeing something good. Like, for example, a Wilson's Petrel. You can imagine how they felt. So could we. We left them setting up on the port side for the return journey. It wouldn't surprise me if they're still there.

Tony and I drove off the ferry, contemplating how cruel bird-watching can be. But we weren't going to let it spoil our holiday. We had a feeling we were 'on a roll', and the next day proved it. At Tacumshin Lake there were twenty-five species of waders, including no fewer than five 'Yanks'. Not five birds – five species. And only one of them didn't have a little friend or two with them. There were four Pectoral Sandpipers, three Baird's Sandpipers, two Buff-breasted Sandpipers, two Wilson's Phalaropes, and a lone Semipalmated Sandpiper. It may well have been the most impressive collection of American waders ever seen this side of the Atlantic. As an added bonus, we were treated to a demonstration of the finer points of 'Semi P' identification by Killian Mullarney, complete with instant illustrations. If you are not familiar with Killian's work, you should be, and I dare say you soon will be. He is, I believe, probably at this very moment, working on the plates for some new and even more authoritative field guide, if he isn't leading a 'guided' bird tour somewhere. Back at Tacumshin that day, we had the privilege of our own personal guided tour round the feather detail of Semipalmated Sandpipers as compared with Little Stints. I have absolutely no intention of pontificating about it here. It is an awfully esoteric topic which would bore and boggle all but the most ardent shorebird aficionado, but I am absolutely certain that a complete non-birder would have been utterly fascinated to witness Killian at work 'in the field'.

Drummers talk about having to have 'co-ordinated independence', or is it 'independent co-ordination'? What it means is the ability to play different rhythms on different parts of the drum kit with each limb. Left foot on the 'high-hat', right foot on the bass drum, left hand on the snare, right hand on the cymbals. It seems to me that bird artists need to have similar abilities. Killian certainly has.

Scilly, sometime in the early-1970s . . . note the standard 'Beatle' haircut.

Robin Hemming . . . with the one that *didn't* get away.

Typical 'guided tour' clients. Probably discussing warbler wing formulae, or possibly where to buy a nice cream tea.

'The Scilly Birdman' himself, David Hunt.

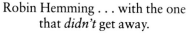

'No walking'. OK, but how about 'running like the clappers'?

So, if you saw a tiger's 'pug mark', would *you* go for a stroll in the jungle?

The gentle side of India. Corbett National Park.

One of the wonders of the world – a man managing to ignore the Taj Mahal! Must be a bird-watcher. 1979.

This is how they go tiger watching these days . . . which is probably why you don't often see one!

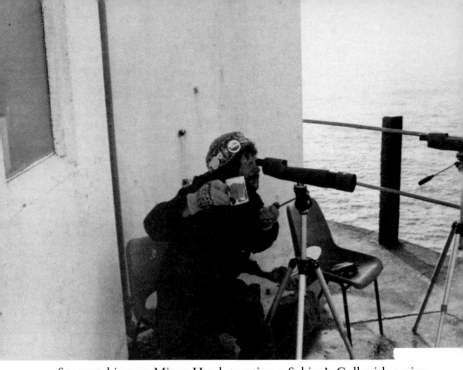

Sea-watching on Mizen Head, toasting a Sabine's Gull with a nice
'cup of filth'.

The aftermath at Tacumshin. So, how many Irishmen does it take to
rescue two stupid Englishmen?

Shetland landscape – bleak but beautiful. The tiny walled gardens are called 'planticrews'. I once found a Great Reed Warbler in this one.

The launch of a new boat – cause for island celebration. A few weeks later it sank – and they celebrated again!

The island 'Heligoland Trap' on the main valley wall. Note recycled Christmas trees, much appreciated by rare birds.

Two sheep on one rope – discussing whose turn it is to panic.

Laura . . . looking suitably enchanted with the idea of honeymoon-
ing in Papua New Guinea.

This tribal chief was also the local bank manager. Beats a bowler hat
and pinstripes, I'd say.

I tried to add a little spice to the honeymoon by donning rubber-wear. It didn't work.

The campsite on Mount Missim. Offering complete protection against head hunters and falling trees. *Not*.

He kept one eye looking through his telescope and the other on his sketch-pad, which he held in his left hand whilst drawing with his right, whilst at the same time keeping his ears alert for any unfamiliar calls, whilst also giving us a feather-by-feather commentary. If his drawings had been merely half-finished field sketches I would have been impressed enough, but in fact they were more detailed than photographs! Watching Killian at word added immeasurably to the 'Tacumshin experience' that day. As indeed did the almost orgasmic combination of fish and chips, washed down with Irish whiskey, consumed under the stars that evening. Heaven knows, I've tried to convey the magic of that moment to Laura many times, but she remains utterly insensitive, to the point of sarcasm: 'Oh, go on Bill ... DO tell us the Irish fish and chips story.' I guess you had to be there.

Apart from enthralling us with his fieldcraft, Killian gave us advice on where to spend the rest of our week. 'There's obviously a lot of "Yanks" around' – obviously! – 'but I don't think anybody's checked out Lissagriffin lately.'

Now this statement was a measure of just how delightfully under-watched Ireland could be. Lissagriffin is a brackish lough right down at the very south-west corner of the country. It is about as near to America as you can get without swimming, and obviously 'should be good' for American waders. Nearby is Mizen Head, a superb sea-watching promontory. There are also gardens to check for small birds, and breeding Choughs on the local cliffs. All in all, the area is a birding hot spot if ever there was one. In England – or, no doubt, in America – it would be overrun with birders most days throughout the autumn. But not in Ireland in the early eighties. The idea that 'no one had checked it lately' was like a bugle-call to action for Tony and me: 'Go west, young men.' Or middle-aged men, anyway.

Lissagriffin duly produced its Yanks: five Buff-breasts, a Pec (Pectoral Sandpiper), and an American (Lesser) Golden Plover. Having counted, admired and photographed the waders, we went in search of seabirds. Mizen Head looks like something out of legend. It is a craggy finger of land pointing out into the Atlantic – next stop, America. The moorland on top is bleak and heathery, the cliffs alongside huge. You can drive out as far as an iron gate. Here you have to park and continue on foot. The track winds down to a narrow bridge which crosses a vast rocky chasm, at the bottom of which the sea swirls and roars like something out of a Viking saga. You feel there ought to be a troll guarding the bridge (would that make it a troll-bridge?), or a big fat opera singer with horns on her head belting out an aria to the wind. At the very least, you expect to be greeted by Indiana Jones.

In fact, on that particular September day, we were greeted by the lighthouse-keeper, a rotund Irishman with a complexion like leather, who welcomed Tony as an old friend (which he was) and invited us to stay. Anyone who has sat getting soaked sea-watching out on a headland will appreciate what a wonderful offer it was. Our room was as spartan as a prison cell, but what a view! We set up our telescopes at the window, and in the morning we only had to prop ourselves up on our pillows to be able to peer out at the ocean. Not only that, but we were woken by the lighthouse-keeper with mugs of hot tea. Well, I say 'tea' … in fact, we'd found it a lot easier to identify the Wilson's Petrel than whatever that brew was. Its consistency was somewhere between cocoa and mud. Tony christened it 'a nice cup of filth'. Of course, he meant it in a caring way. And so did the lighthouse-keeper. And anyway, whatever it looked like, it tasted terrific. Mind you, most things taste terrific when you're toasting a fly-past of Sooty, Great, and Cory's Shearwaters.

It seemed we just couldn't lose on this trip. On our final morning at the lighthouse we awoke to find the wind had switched round from west to east. Surely this meant a big 'dip' in the sea-watching (to coin a birding phrase)? Not at all. Four Sabine's Gulls flapped past, as if to guide us back to County Cork. We followed their directions, and found that, at every estuary we crossed, the easterly had brought in packs of Black Terns. At Ballycotton there were more 'Yanks' still in residence: three Pectoral Sandpipers, another Wilson's Phalarope, and one or maybe two Semipalmated Sandpipers. As a final flourish, whilst sorting out the 'peeps', I picked up a Kentish Plover, which was, in fact, even scarcer in Ireland than a 'Semi P'.

At this point I had to fly back to London from Cork. My only worry was that I was leaving Tony – who was able to stay on for a few more days – possibly to 'grip me off'. No doubt he tried. At Ballycotton, he confirmed the presence of no fewer than three Semi Ps, and, back at Tacumshin, he added Long-billed Dowitcher and several more Buff-breasts (bringing the flock up to nine!), but not the 'crippler' he was probably hoping for. When he got home, he rang to tell me how he'd got on. 'It was great,' he said, 'but', – and I admit I was almost a little touched by this – 'it wasn't quite the same being on my own.'

Aha ... another bird-watcher confessing that he's human after all!

'Then we must do Ireland again,' I resolved. And we did.

In fact, Tony went one better – he took a job over there. He was actually based in Belfast but, come the autumns, he migrated south in his Dormobile. I flew over to join him, and we worked our way across Wexford, Cork and Kerry. I'd like to think that we earned the respect of the Irish bird-watchers by finding quite a few good birds, but, if we did, it didn't extend to their resisting giving us rather facetious nicknames. It has since come to my notice that we were referred to as 'Laurel and Hardy', 'Little and Large', and even 'the Odd Couple'. I shall take that last one as some kind of word-play on my surname, rather than a comment on our sexuality. Actually, I suppose it is a perfectly fair assessment of what we looked like. The undeniable fact is that Tony is very very tall and thin. And I'm not. OK. I'm small and plump. A classic comedy duo, if ever there was one. Besides which, if we did ever have pretensions to dignity, they were entirely destroyed by the events of one fateful day in September 1984 at Tacumshin Lake.

First, let me describe Tacumshin Lake. It's big – very big. The whole area is probably at least a couple of miles long, and a mile across. It lies just behind the 'sea wall', though in fact this is a high shingle bank, largely cut off by deep channels, and is, in any case, so steep and hard to climb that in all the times I've been there I've never actually seen the sea. Access is much easier at various points along the north shore of the lake. Here you can approach along a narrow road, park, and make your way down to the shoreline. Before you get there, you will no doubt be distracted by enticing areas of reed-beds or marshy ponds. These make an excellent habitat for swamp-loving birds, which may include anything from harriers to 'marsh terns'. Stretching out beyond this is the main lake itself, except that the water is still quite a long way away, across a vast expanse of sand. On a sunny day it always reminds me of a mirage in a desert. It's also very similar to those salt flats – in Nevada, are they? – where reckless people make attempts at land-speed records. However, all this adds to the convenience of the place. The sands are extremely firm, and you can drive a vehicle across them quite safely. For many years, this has been the 'traditional' way of doing Tacumshin. Unless there have been very heavy rains, the narrow tarmac road that

approaches from the west gives way to an equally well
defined and well worn track, which takes you out nearly a
mile across the solid sands until you eventually reach the
water's edge. Once there, the immediate outlook may
appear bleak, but if you drive around slowly you'll
eventually come across packs of waders either feeding or
roosting. Amongst these can be all kinds of rarities.
Fortunately, as most birders know, birds seem to find a car
no more threatening than a cow. So that's the way to
watch. From inside a car, I mean. It's much cosier than on
cow-back (not that I've ever tried that).

So ... picture it, if you will. Early one September
morning, Tony and I drive down the narrow lane to
Tacumshin Lake in the Dormobile. We pause briefly at the
marshy area. A couple of Pectoral Sandpipers fly over,
calling. Good start. Full of optimism, we drive off across
the sands. There has been little recent rain, so the track is
nice and firm. No problems. Eventually, we approach the
edge of the water. We stop and scan. We spot a pack of
waders and drive over to them: Dunlin, Little Stints.
Nothing unusual. Another scan ... another little flock.
Drive over to them. There's quite a lot to sort through
here, but, after a good scrutiny, we have to conclude
there's still nothing rare. Never mind, take our time. We've
got all morning before we are due to set off back
northwards. We decide to drive over to an area of dry
marsh, often favoured by Buff-breasts.

Tony starts the engine again, and puts his foot on the
accelerator. But we don't move. He tries again. This time
we are aware of that ominous whirring sound that
suggests that at least one wheel is going round, but not
actually getting anywhere. I get out to assess the situation.
Years of birding have made me quite observant. I
immediately notice that the van is not quite level. This is
because the back left-side wheel has gouged itself a snug

little channel in the apparently perfectly dry sand. No problem. I suggest that Tony tries backing instead. He does. The van becomes even less level as the wheel snuggles further down in what is now beginning to look a bit more like a shallow pit of mud. OK. Don't panic. We've got some old blankets in the back of the Dormobile. Admittedly they are supposed to be our bedclothes, but I guess we can wash them later. For half an hour I rummage away under the tyres, stuffing in blankets, anoraks, smelly socks, and anything else that might persuade the van to 'get a grip'. But eventually we have to face it: we are well and truly stuck.

It wasn't actually a dangerous situation. Although the miles of sand and the water's edge may *look* like the seashore, it isn't. So we weren't about to get stranded by the tide. We were simply stuck. If it had been the weekend, there might have been a few other birders driving around – on the perfectly safe sands! – who could have given us a pull or a push. But it was Monday. There wasn't a soul in sight.

'OK. I'll walk back to the nearest farm,' volunteered Tony. 'I'm sure there's one back along the road.'

I was sure there was one too, though 'back along the road' was about three miles away. Tony set off across the sands, whilst I stayed to guard the Dormobile. Looking back on it now, why on earth I felt I needed to guard the van I really don't know. I mean, it was hardly likely that there'd be any passing car thieves, who just happened to be taking a stroll in the middle of Tacumshin Lake. I suspect the real reason I didn't keep Tony company was that I was hoping to spot a rarity whilst he was away. I don't get out birding so often that I was going to waste time traipsing around looking for friendly farmers. Added to which, Tony was now living in Ireland, so he'd speak the language. (Well, understand the accent.)

About two hours later, I still hadn't found a rare bird, but I did spot a small tractor chugging over the horizon. On board were Tony and an archetypal cheery Irish farmer. He took one look at the Dormobile and immediately assessed the situation: 'Ah, you're stuck.'

Had he only just realized? Maybe Tony's command of Irish dialect wasn't so good after all. Anyway, clearly the farmer was here to help, and he was immediately reassuring: 'Ah, 'tis no problem. It happens all the time.'

We admired his self-restraint. He could easily have added: 'To stupid English bird-watchers.' But he didn't. He didn't even allow himself a derisive chuckle. What he did do was tie a rope to the front of our van and attach the other end to the back of his tractor. Then he revved up noisily. The tractor strained. At first nothing seemed to be happening. Then we realized that, though the van wasn't moving, the tractor was. Not forwards, but downwards. The more it strained, the lower it sank. We yelled, but the farmer couldn't hear us above the noise of his own engine. Suddenly, it juddered into silence. He dismounted, stood back to survey his tractor, and announced his verdict.

'Ah. It's stuck.'

We looked suitably bemused. He reassured us again.

'Ah, 'tis no problem. It happens all the time.'

It was our turn not to make sarky comments.

This time Tony stayed to guard the van. I trudged off back across the sands with the farmer. An hour later, we arrived at the farm.

'We're going to need a bigger tractor,' he declared.

I agreed, but I couldn't see any bigger tractors in the yard. clearly this could be going to take some time. I was beginning to get a little perturbed, for I absolutely had to be back in England early the next morning as I was filming for the BBC. Looking back, I think it was at this moment that I made a crucial mistake. I conveyed my concern to the farmer.

'Look, I need to call the BBC,' I explained.

'Ah. You'd better use the phone then. Otherwise they won't hear you.'

I smiled at his flippancy, whilst thinking that he had no reason to get too cocky, since his tractor was stuck out there as well. Anyway, I rang the BBC and explained that I just might be late back for filming. I certainly didn't tell them that I was in Ireland, stranded out in the middle of two miles of mudflats.

'Did you get through to the BBC?' asked the farmer.

'Yes, thank you,' I replied.

He seemed pleased. He took the phone, and I left him making calls. Within twenty minutes or so we were both perched on another – much bigger – tractor, along with another farmer who was either the tractor's owner, or someone who wanted a good laugh.

Another hour later, we trundled up to Tony. He was still guarding the van, whilst scanning the waders. This time the two farmers decided to discuss the dilemma before leaping in, as it were.

'We don't want it to happen again, do we?'

We all agreed on that.

'What I think we should do,' the second farmer suggested, 'is *test* the mud.'

It seemed like a good idea. I started to wander around, stamping and jumping up and down. 'It *seems* pretty firm.'

'Ah yes, but ...' interrupted the farmer, 'it might be all right for a person ... but ...'

At which point, he boarded his tractor and began to edge forward.

'What are you doing?' I asked.

'I'm going to test the mud,' he explained.

Tony and I looked at each other as if to say: 'Well ... I suppose they know what they're doing.' We watched as the tractor drove across one patch of apparently safe sand.

'Well, this bit seems all right,' came the farmer's verdict. He tested another area. 'And this bit seems solid enough.' He scanned the sands. Suddenly, his eyes narrowed. 'Ah ... now *that* bit looks a little bit soft.'

And to prove it ... he drove straight across it, and sank up to the axles.

So that was one Dormobile and *two* tractors stuck in the middle of Tacumshin Lake. Tony and I were literally speechless.

The farmer consoled us: 'Ah, 'tis no problem. It happens all the time.'

This time, we both stayed to guard the van. We watched the farmers disappear over the horizon. Two more hours went by. By this time it was late afternoon, and the light was beginning to fade. Never for one moment did it occur to us that the farmers could have just left us there till the next day, or indeed till the next week. In fact, we could have been there still! But the Irish don't treat visitors like that. Sure enough, as we strained our ears for Pectoral Sandpiper calls, we heard instead the comforting rumble of yet another tractor approaching over the horizon. Surely this one would be specially suited to the job? Yes, it was heavy and chunky, a real little juggernaut. Tony and I just stood and admired it as it chugged closer and closer, veered past us, swung to the left, drove round and round in ever-decreasing circles, and ... literally screwed itself into the mud. We didn't say a word. We felt we knew what the reply would be: 'Ah, 'tis no problem. It happens all the time.'

The day was nearly done. I really had to get back to London somehow. I set off with the farmers. After about half a mile I stopped and looked back. A blood-red sun was setting behind three tractors and a Dormobile, lying at grotesque angles and casting bizarre shadows across the sands. It looked like the scene after the last battle of

'Desert Storm'. There really should have been some wistful eerie film music playing. Instead – and I don't know why I remember this so clearly – the farmers were marching along singing Stevie Wonder's 'I Just Called To Say I Love You'! Surreal, or what?

Back at the farm, I thanked the farmers and bade them farewell. They assured me that Tony would be quite safe sleeping out there in the middle of the lake surrounded by three tractors, and that they'd go back to try again first thing the next morning. I hitched a lift to Wexford, caught a train to Dublin, and just managed to leap onto the last plane back to London. After my next day's filming with the BBC, I raced home and sat expectantly by the phone, waiting for the call that I knew had to come. 'Ring, ring.' It was Tony. I knew there weren't any phones in the middle of Tacumshin Lake, so that was a hopeful sign. He was calling from Belfast.

'So what happened?' I asked eagerly. He told me.

He had spent a perfectly comfortable night out there in the middle of the lake. No one had tried to pinch the Dormobile, or any of the tractors. Then, even as the sun had risen in the east, bathed in its glowing light, out of the dawn and over the horizon had lumbered the biggest mechanical grab you ever did see. It was as huge as a dinosaur, with caterpillar tracks so that it didn't sink, and an enormous 'bucket' thing on the end of its neck. I have to confess that I was half hoping Tony was going to say that it too had got stuck. But no. It had opened its massive jaws and literally lifted each tractor, and the van, out of the mud, and plonked them back on dry sand.

OK. Drama over. But there remained the little matter of 'the bill'. At various times during the day, whilst waiting for the next tractor to come and get stuck, we had conjectured about how much this was all going to cost. Somehow, we rather doubted that Tony's car insurance covered getting stuck in the middle of a lake whilst bird-watching. We had ended up having to hire about a hundred tons of 'heavy plant': three tractors and a monster mechanical grab! OK, maybe it could be argued that if the first tractor had been better suited to the job, then the other two wouldn't have got stuck, but that seemed rather ungracious. Tony decided to trust to Irish generosity. He approached the famer who owned the first tractor, and who seemed to be in charge of the operation.

'So ... er ... how much do we owe you, then?'

'Well ...' replied the farmer, as if considering how to break rather bad news, 'it is an awful lot of machinery.'

'Yes ... I know,' agreed Tony. 'So ... er ...?'

'So ... er ... it's going to be pretty expensive.'

Tony looked understandably worried. The farmer took a deep breath, no doubt preparing to announce a very large sum.

But before I reveal the 'damage', remember I said I thought that I might have made a mistake when I asked to make that phone call back at the farm? Well, proof was at hand.

'So how much?' asked Tony.

'Well, it certainly won't be cheap. Still, never mind ...' continued the farmer, as if he was about to soften the blow '... the BBC are paying, aren't they?'

'Are they?' asked Tony, no doubt strung somewhere between relief and total puzzlement.

'Yes,' confirmed the farmer. 'I heard Mr Oddie call the BBC. Are you making a film here, then?'

Tony explained that we were not in fact a wealthy BBC film crew, but a couple of relatively impecunious bird-watchers who were no doubt destined to become the laughing-stock of the whole of Ireland. The farmer was sympathetic. They settled for 100 Irish punts, which in those days was even less than its English equivalent. It was a pretty reasonable charge for hiring enough machinery to resurface the M25.

Thus ended the ultimate Irish joke featuring two stupid Englishmen. Throughout the episode the Irish farmers were cheeriness and courtesy itself. But I can't help wondering if one of them was also very canny. I've got a sneaky feeling that, once he'd heard me make that call to London, he'd been on the phone to every farmer in County Wexford, saying: 'Quick, get your tractor over to Tacumshin. The BBC are paying!'

Oh, by the way, there was a consolation. Some time between tractors two and three ... we found a Semipalmated Sandpiper! Moreover, Tacumshin is still as magical as ever. But if you go there ... I suggest you walk.

5
The Road to the Isles
Shetland

SHETLAND
* ESPECIALLY
OUT SKERRIES

the 70's.

BLACK BROWED ALBATROSS
('Albert'- wishing he/she was a Gannet?)
Hermaness.

Wind blown
WILLOW WARBLER
(wishing he'd stayed
in Africa!)

EIDER DRAKES + sleepy duck
("oo~oo~oo" call- sounds like shocked
old lady!)

Blue

The "wee black + white bird
on the washing line"

red

male
BLUETHROAT
(Disgruntled, cos he's not in colour.)

male COLLARED
FLYCATCHER

ARCTIC
TERN   chowdby

ARCTIC
SKUA

chowdby   BONXIE.....

A quick geography lesson. The Northern Isles are to the north.

Of Britain, that is. Heading towards the Arctic from England, you pass over Scotland. Then there's a bit of sea, then comes the first group of Northern Isles, Orkney (or the Orkneys, if you prefer, as indeed there are a lot of them.) From the northern tip of Orkney there's another fair expanse of sea – about 40 miles – till you get to the southern tip of the next archipelago, Shetland, or the Shetlands (there's a lot of those, too). Orkney covers a fair old area. So does Shetland. But half-way between the two is a single tiny island: Fair Isle. Whoever named it was probably being sarcastic as, from a distance, it appears to be little more than a bleak oversized rock, set in treacherous waters that have claimed many a ship. On the other hand, it does have a couple of small sheltered harbours – or 'havens' – so perhaps Fair Isle was in fact christened by an appreciative mariner after a rough day of being tossed on the stormy waters where the North Sea meets the Atlantic. And days don't come much rougher than that. Anyway, forgive me if you know all this. It's just that, though most people have heard of Fair Isle – either on the shipping forecast or as a knitting pattern – not everyone knows exactly where it is. Unless you've been there. And if you *have* been there, it's pretty likely that you are a bird-watcher. In which case, you'll also know that Fair Isle is the site of a long-established bird observatory, and one of the most wondrous places on earth for marvelling at seabirds, and for studying migration, and –

perhaps most exciting of all – for finding rare birds.

I first visited Fair Isle in 1959, when I was eighteen. Over subsequent years I returned several times, and it never failed to provide memorable experiences of birds, birding and birders. I could tell many a yarn about Fair Isle, but not now. I want to cover something a little different. That was also exactly what I attempted to do in May 1975: cover something a little different. The relevance to Fair Isle is this: back in the sixties and seventies a visit to the island always involved making a crossing, either by boat or small plane, from the southern tip of Shetland. Eventually it dawned on me that if a tiny island could pull in so many migrants, it was fairly likely that a whacking great archipelago, only 20 miles away, would probably attract even more. OK, they might be a bit spread out and less easy to find, but there had to be various favoured hot spots on 'mainland' Shetland (which is actually called 'Mainland'). It hardly took a genius to work this out, and indeed there were a few local bird-watchers who were no doubt perfectly aware of it and covered their own various local patches. However, to a southerner such as I, the lure of Fair Isle was so irresistible that I had never lingered on Mainland any longer than it took to leap on the boat or plane. I had once been delayed for an hour and found a Richard's Pipit in a field near the airport. I had also noticed, when browsing through back numbers of the Shetland Bird Report, that several rarities had turned up in the garden of the nearby Sumburgh Hotel. They'd presumably also been found by delayed Fair-Isle-bound birders, or possibly by locals who knew full well that Mainland was potentially every bit as prolific as the magic isle.

Anyway, the message finally got home to me in 1970. I was returning from Fair Isle after what was then – and possibly still is – arguably the most spectacular spring fall the island had ever enjoyed. There had literally been cascades of chats and warblers and, on the peak day, counts of nearly fifty each of Wrynecks and Bluethroats. There had also been several rarities, including four Thrush Nightingales, and Little and Spotted Crakes in the same ditch on the same morning. But, like I said, that's another story. Meanwhile, by the day I left the island, things had gone fairly quiet. However, back at Sumburgh, in the mere half-hour or so that I had to 'waste' waiting for my plane back to London, I found no fewer than five Bluethroats, a Corncrake, and an assortment of common migrants, hardly without stepping beyond the airport perimeter. Maybe Mainland kept its birds longer, I mused. I could also only wonder about what kind of invasion there had been a few days earlier, when Fair Isle was almost sinking under the weight of migrants. As I checked in (or out, rather) at the glorified wooden hut that passed as an airport terminal, I vowed to return as soon as possible, and try that 'something a little different' I've already alluded to. Unfortunately – or fortunately – my TV career rather took off in the early seventies, and five more years went by. Until ...

... May 1975. My birding companion on the trip was Andrew Lowe, with whom I had shared many formative years of studying and suffering one of the world's least charismatic local patches: the concrete-sided and almost birdless Bartley Reservoir, on the edge of Birmingham. I have always argued that the almost fail-safe thrill of regular-patch watching is that any species that is new for your patch is by definition a rarity and is therefore exciting. Logically, then, the ideal local patch would be one that has no birds on it whatsoever, so that if anything at all turns up, you will be immensely grateful. Bartley was almost as bad – or good – as that. For Andy and me our Bartley years had been very character-forming; a bit like graduating from an ornithological Outward Bound school. (I did in fact spend a month at an Outward Bound school, whose motto then was: 'When it hurts, it's doing you good'. I often told myself that at Bartley.) Anyway, the result was that Andy and I were certainly no strangers to taking risks. Namely, in this case, the risk of visiting Shetland, but *not* going over to Fair Isle.

We had a plan. We could check into the stately old Sumburgh Hotel with its famous garden. We hadn't bothered to book. We didn't figure that early May would be the peak holiday season up in Shetland, if indeed there was any holiday season at all. The hotel would be our base – our very own temporary bird observatory – from which we would spend the week methodically covering the area round the southern tip of Mainland. There was a considerable variety of habitat, including several areas of marsh and fresh water, as well as the various crops, cliffs and shorelines: plenty of ground to cover and an excellent chance of finding some good birds. Thus, late on the afternoon of 7 May, as we came in to land at Sumburgh Airport, I was full of optimism and Andy was full of anticipation. He'd never been to Shetland before. I hadn't been for five years. What neither of us appreciated was that, in those five years, something rather important had happened to Shetland. A little word with a big impact. Oil.

The first shock occurred before we'd even come down on the runaway. As we circled over the south, I began pointing out some of the likely birdy areas. 'There's the lighthouse on Sumburgh Head. Good seabird colonies on the cliffs there. Maybe the light attracts night migrants. And that's Scatness. There's a couple of little pools on there, could be good for wildfowl. And that's Pool of Virkie. It's tidal, excellent for waders, and there's some lovely little ditches with patches of willows in them. That's where I had five Bluethroats this time in 1970. It's right by the airstrip, but that's no problem, it's only a tiny little airport, the terminal's just a wooden....' My voice tailed off as we swooped down towards what looked like a cross between Heathrow, a military base, and a building-site. 'Oh,' I observed. 'It's changed.'

It certainly had. What had been a little wooden hut was now a great big concrete terminal. Inside it, instead of being greeted by a couple of cheery Shetlanders and a whiff of sea air, we had to push through a loose scrum of oilmen, emitting their own atmosphere of cigarette smoke and whisky fumes. What's more, the voices certainly didn't have the Shetland lilt. There were heavy Scots, various Scandinavian, even English accents. I was perturbed. I mean, I don't want to sound racist, but when I went to Shetland I liked to hear the Shetland brogue – which owes far more to Norway than Scotland – and I wanted to be told 'Ah, 'tis a fine day', rather than have to listen to babble about refineries and pipelines. I didn't like what had happened to the terminal. Even the little newspaper kiosk had grown to the size of a proper newsagent, complete with a top shelf full of 'girlie mags', presumably for the comfort of those men destined to spend the next month on the oil-rigs. Alongside was a selection of frilly underwear for the men to take back to their wives or girlfriends, to make sure they were in the mood to give them what they'd been missing. Well, I presume that was the idea. Heaven knows, it must get lonely out there, so I suppose a little cross-dressing might brighten up the nights on the rigs. The notion of an oil-rigger wearing a push-up bra cheered me up a little and revived my optimism. I tried to reassure myself: 'It'll be fine once we get out of here.'

But it wasn't fine. We emerged to a cacophony. All around us dumper trucks and tractors were busy expanding the airport complex as noisily as possible. Above us there was the constant roaring and rattling of helicopters ferrying men and equipment. I yelled to Andy that I'd 'once seen Richard's Pipit in the field across the road'. This information was obliterated by a din that would have drowned out a town-crier with a megaphone. Again I tried to think positive: 'Birds don't really mind noise,' I told myself.

'But I do,' I couldn't help adding.

At least the racket receded a little as we set off towards the Sumburgh Hotel. This turned out to be a longer walk than I recalled, largely because the once-direct route was now 'out of bounds', and we had to traipse all the way round the new airport perimeter road, which skirted a formidable new fence with several 'No Entry' signs on it. Clearly restricted access was going to be another problem. Never mind, there was always the famous Sumburgh Hotel garden. As it turned out, this was a walled patch hardly bigger than a tennis-court, with no visible vegetation in it except a row of extremely stunted sycamore bushes, cringing from the northern winds and, at this time of the year, bearing not a single leaf. I had a worrying recollection that most of the best birds had turned up in there in autumn, when there may well have been foliage to hide in and seeds to feed on. In early May, the garden looked, well, unpromising. Nevertheless, the spirit of Bartley Reservoir shone through.

'If we're staying at the hotel, we'll be able to do the garden every morning,' I announced defiantly. 'I bet we get something.' We did. We got turned away. The hotel was full. This despite the fact that it had recently acquired an 'extension', in the unsightly shape of a 'new block' whose Portakabin-style architecture matched the stately grey stone of the main building about as sensitively as a satellite dish on the Taj Mahal. Every room had been booked by oil companies for the foreseeable future. We would have to find somewhere else to stay. The manager was sympathetic, and offered us the use of his phone so that we could let our fingers to the walking.

Our feet had to do quite a bit of walking as well. It was more or less dark when, having filled up on pork pies and brown ale, we trudged up to the front door of what was advertised as a 'Guest House', but looked more like an elongated prefabricated garage. It had presumably been designed by the same architect responsible for the Sumburgh Hotel extension. His sense of insulation was no better than his sense of aesthetics. The walls were paper thin, which meant that not only was our room freezing cold, but we could also hear the oilman 'next door' keeping warm. This he did by slowly drinking himself into a stupor. It started with a lot of clonking, glugging and gasping. Then progressed to singing. Then vomiting, and finally to snoring, which kept us awake most of the night, until the whining of the first helicopter of the day told us it was time to get up.

We spent the morning of 8 May thoroughly covering our designated local patch and searching for migrants. We came up with one Willow Warbler. If I close my eyes I can still see that poor bedraggled little bird, clinging to the top rung of a barbed-wire fence, wondering whether to end it all by impaling itself rather than suffer another minute shivering in the icy wind, under a grey pitiless sky in which – in place of the insects it craved – the only flying things were monstrous helicopters that nearly blew it off its perch every time one roared overhead. I know birds aren't supposed to mind noise, but I don't think they actually like it. I was beginning to hate it. This just wasn't the island ambience I knew and cherished. Birdless was bad enough, but noisy and ugly ... this was sacrilege.

I was not enjoying myself. I was beginning to be racked by a depressing feeling that the holiday was doomed. I've always been prone to overwhelming pangs of pessimism and, under such circumstances, I have been known to resort to rather over-dramatic gestures, such as giving up and going home. But one can only inflict such abject defeatism on oneself. I could hardly suggest to Andy that he should pack in his first visit to Shetland after half a day! A rather more tempting solution was, tantalizingly, almost visible on the horizon. On a clear day from the Sumburgh shore you can see Fair Isle. It was probably a good thing that poor visibility was keeping it hidden that morning, otherwise I rather suspect we'd have been off there as soon as possible. Or was it that we rang up and the observatory was full? In any event, we made a decision. We would get a bus to Lerwick (Shetland's main town), hire a car, and go and explore the whole of Mainland. Or, more specifically, we intended to drive off northwards and get as far away from the airport as possible.

Several hours and two car ferries later, we landed on the island of Unst. A couple more hours after that we were striding towards the most northerly point in Britain! That's what I call escaping. Not that there wasn't a price to pay. The skua colony on Hermaness is no place for the faint-hearted. Both Arctic and Great Skuas defend their territory by soaring up to a great height, then dive-bombing you at a ferocious speed. The Great Skuas rejoice in the local name of 'Bonxies', which I dare say they acquired because they attempt to bonk you (in the strictly non-erotic sense). I've never heard of anyone actually being struck by a Bonxie, but this is no doubt because a human being's instinctive reaction to seeing a bird with a six-foot wing span and a wicked gleam in its eye plummeting towards one like a kamikaze pilot, is either to run like hell, or dig a six-foot trench and leap into it. It made our progress across Hermaness a slow process, but being bonked by skuas was infinitely preferable to being buzzed by helicopters, and anyway it's what you have to do if you want to visit Albert.

Albert is an Albatross. Albert Ross – get it? Well, he was named back in the early 1970s, when ornithological humour wasn't terribly inventive. Amazingly, even as I write, I have just read in Recent Bird News that Albert has returned to his outcrop on Unst for the twenty-third year. Albert is the only Black-browed Albatross on Hermaness. He may well be the only Black-browed Albatross in the northern hemisphere, since most of his chums live down near the Antarctic. Presumably his compass has been reversed and he thinks the Shetlands are the Falklands. Not only is his sense of direction highly suspect, but so is his ability to identify other birds. He may be very old but he can't be very observant, as he doesn't seem to have noticed that he is surrounded entirely by Gannets. This wouldn't really matter if it wasn't for certain signs that Albert would like to start a family. As it happens, Albert may even be a female, as he, she, or it has been scraping what appears to be a nest. Alas, it is likely that Albert will remain wide-eyed and eggless, as the chances of two Black-browed Albatrosses getting so spectacularly disorientated must be very slim indeed. And there are no records of Gannets and Albatrosses hybridizing. It's sad, really: twenty-three years sitting on a cold rock without nooky, and likely to remain so. Worse than working on an oil-rig. As we admired Albert, I rather wished I could drop down a girlie mag or some frilly underwear. Whatever turned him/her on. Ah well, maybe he appreciated the peace and quiet.

We certainly did.

In fact, we stayed enjoying the ambience just those vital few minutes too long. By the time we'd debated Albert's sexuality, crawled back through the skuas, driven back across Unst – pausing to admire a field full of wheatears – we screeched on to the quay just in time to see the last ferry

docking ... on the other side. It didn't really bother us.
There are far worse places to have to spend the night than
amid the lovely green wildness of Unst, but it *is* more
comfortable in a bed. Unfortunately, like the rest of
Shetland, Unst seemed to be full. We ended up knocking
pathetically on doors, until a kindly householder offered
us a bed in her spare room. It was exactly that: a bed. Just
one. And a single bed at that. Heaven knows, our Bartley
ordeals had brought Andy and me pretty close, but not
that close.

The bed was cosy, and the carpet was soft enough, and
we didn't have a vomiting oilman next door. We slept
well. Albert had cheered us up, and we set out on the 9th
in good spirits. By the end of the day, they had been pretty
thoroughly dampened. Literally. In ever-deteriorating
weather, we worked our way back southwards. My
notebook of the time tells the rather unmemorable story:

'Wind northerly. Wet.

Unst: A few Arctic Terns by the ferry.

Yell (the next island): Two Black-tailed Godwits.' And,
finally, back at ...

'Sumburgh: One Robin.'

At least it was in the famous Sumburgh Hotel garden.

Not a great day. That evening, at the paper-walled
garage we called home, we made a phone call to one of the
relatively few Shetland birders to see if anything had been
seen anywhere else on the islands. It had. A female
Wilson's Phalarope – not only rare, but very beautiful –
had been reported from Strand Loch. 'When?' That
afternoon. 'And exactly where is Strand Loch?' Near
Tingwall.

We looked at the map. There it was: Strand Loch, a tiny
patch of water, right by the road. We must have driven
straight past it!

It was another noisy night at the 'garage', but it wasn't

the oilman that kept us awake. It was the possibility of seeing a major rarity. We were up with the dawn and, within less than an hour, were sitting in the car, sheltering from the rain and scanning the shores of Strand Loch. A Wilson's Phalarope in breeding plumage is a veritable harlequin of a bird. Not only are its colours varied, subtle and exquisite, but it looks as if it's been designed by Picasso. Moreover, and almost uniquely in the bird world, it is the female that is the more impressive of the pair. Yes indeed, to use twitching parlance, a female Wilson's Phalarope in full nuptial dress is most certainly a 'crippler'.

Unfortunately, it wasn't there. What's more, Strand Loch is so small that we didn't even experience the suspense of searching. The disappointment was instant. It took about two minutes to be absolutely certain that the bird had flown, even though we sat for over an hour hoping it would come back. Apparently it did, eventually. But not till the following year, when it (or its sister) visited another part of Shetland, presumably having spent the winter the wrong side of the Atlantic. Maybe it was using the same compass as Albert.

Meanwhile, we spent another dire and increasingly desperate morning searching for migrants, driving round in pelting rain and a howling wind, over an area that is the size of a large English county … It was beginning to dawn on us why so many birders stuck to Fair Isle. Shetland is big. Very big. No doubt masses of birds do turn up there, but finding them is definitely needle-in-a-haystack time. Or it certainly was back in the seventies, way before Birdlines, pagers, and mobile phones. By lunchtime on the 10th, I was suffering a serious midday crisis. I had to get on to a small island. Andrew agreed. We called Fair Isle again. No birds, and no beds. Then I had a brainwave. Maybe it was the fact that the assistant warden on Fair Isle had answered the phone that had jogged my memory.

'Assistant warden' ... I recalled a former assistant who had been present on the island during the great spring fall of 1970: Iain Robertson. He had been so taken by Shetland in general, and small-island life in particular, that he had followed up his Fair Isle job by spending a year on somewhere called Out Skerries. I didn't even know exactly where it was, but I did remember that Iain had seen some very good birds there, eventually really hitting the jackpot by finding Britain's first live Ovenbird in October 1973. (The only previous record had been a single wing found on a beach in Yorkshire in 1969! Not the most logical place for an American bird to be washed up, I would have thought.) We found Out Skerries on the map. It is just about the most easterly island of the Shetland group, promisingly placed indeed. More to the point, it is tiny: even smaller than Fair Isle. Just about the right size for a couple of bird-watchers to cover.

'OK,' we decided, 'Let's go for it.'

'So how do we get there, and where will we stay?'

We called up the contact who'd told us about the Wilson's Phalarope. He wasn't in, which was possibly just as well as he might have gripped us off again. But his silence wasn't going to get us to Skerries, and his was the only name we had. Desperation is a great jogger of memory. I recalled another ex-Fair Isle assistant warden who had gone on to become a doctor somewhere on Shetland. I wasn't sure where, but I did remember his name: Brian Marshall. 'That's funny,' commented Andy, 'I knew a Dr Brian Marshall I was at university with in Newcastle.'

'Was he a bird-watcher?'

'Yes.'

It had to be the same bloke. The coincidence was utterly irresistible; clearly we were meant to follow this up. We found the name in the telephone directory. Dr Brian

Marshall lived on Whalsay, the next island to Out Skerries. What's more, he was in. After Brian and Andy had swapped a few reminiscences about jolly varsity days, we put in our request.

'We'd like to get to Skerries, and we need somewhere to stay.'

'Well,' said Brian. 'there's no boat scheduled today, but I might be able to sort something out. Leave it to me. First, you need to get to Whalsay.'

And to do that, we had to get to Lerwick. Which we did, just in time to leap onto the good ship *Spes Clara,* the characterful – euphemism for a bit battered! – old trawler that served as an inter-island ferry in those days. By this time, the wind was blowing a north-east gale, but you wouldn't have known it as the ship cruised through the relatively calm waters of Lerwick harbour. Then we rounded the headland, and all hell broke loose. Whalsay is north-east of Lerwick, so we were heading straight into the wind. All we could do was hang on and get soaked, which was exhilarating in a masochistic sort of way. At least we were getting there ... slowly! Things calmed down about an hour and a half later as we chugged into the lee of Whalsay and finally docked at the pier at Symbister. Brian was waiting on the quay for us and whisked us up to his house for tea and scones and further bouts of nostalgia, of student days with Andrew and Fair Isle falls with me. Then we were off again. As he drove us back down the jetty Brain explained that the *Spes Clara* wouldn't be continuing to Skerries that day – who could blame it? – but that he'd managed to arrange for one of the island boatmen to take us over in a smaller boat. It certainly was smaller. There was just about room for me, Andy, the skipper, and half a dozen crustaceans. Brian told us that it was normally a lobster boat. Well, it might have been fine for lobsters – presumably they love being tossed about and getting wringing wet – but it wasn't quite so cosy for people. In fact, it was terrifying.

It is extraordinary how there are times in your life when you just have to put your very survival into the hands of a complete stranger. I suppose we do it every time we fly on a plane or go on a bus or in a taxi, but at least under those circumstances you feel pretty certain the person in charge is properly qualified to do the job. But here were Andrew and I, sitting in a glorified rowing boat being hurled around on gigantic waves in a Force 8 gale, steered by a chap whose only nautical expertise that we were aware of was that he owned a couple of lobster pots. We also knew his name. He was called John David. I shall never forget that, partly because they were the only words he spoke in the one and a half hours it took us to make the crossing, and also because I shall always remain deeply grateful to him for getting us there safely. Looking back, I suspect he may have said so little not because he was unsociable, but because he was almost as worried as we were. Or perhaps he was just concentrating. I'm glad he did.

So, we'd made it. It had taken the best part of half a day to get there, but we were on Out Skerries. We couldn't really take in the scenery as we battled up the hill, soaked to the skin and with our heads bowed against the elements. All we really wanted was a warm fire. And we found it. Blazing away in the hearth of 'the chalet'. This was the accommodation that Brian had arranged for us, and frankly it was pretty much ideal for our needs. The building itself was hardly more impressive than our garage-like Guest House, being a very basic, wooden, cube-shaped structure, firmly battened down with steel guy ropes so that it didn't take off in the gales. Inside, however, it looked as if it had been custom-built for birders. There were two bedrooms, with a pleasing plethora of beds: no arguments about who sleeps on the floor here. There was also a shower and loo. All these came off the main room, which had been delightfully designed as lounge, kitchen and 'observation tower'. There were glass doors and several huge windows, so that you could peer out and scan the terrain without actually venturing out into the weather. Mind you, at that moment all the windows were steamed up by the fug of the fire. But that was fine by us. In fact, the chalet belonged to an affluent Shetlander who lived on Mainland, and used it as a holiday home for himself and his family. I don't think he normally rented it out at all. So thank you, Brian. It was brilliant. And it became even better when the lady from the house down the hill popped in 'to make sure we were OK'. She gave us a box full of food, explained how the generator worked, showed us where the coal was kept, and exhorted us to keep the fire well stoked up.

'And if there's anything else you need, just pop down and ask,' she added.

'We could do with some birds,' we grinned.

'Well, it's blowing a nor'easter ... that should bring something,' she predicted.

She was absolutely right. It should. In fact, it had. There was only half an hour's daylight left, and the weather was still pretty foul, but her prophecy inspired us to battle our way down to a sheltered cleft in the cliffs (they call them 'geos' in Shetland). There we found a Common and a Black Redstart, and four Ring Ousels. More migrants than we'd seen on the whole of the trip so far! That evening, we dined on locally caught fresh fish, with neeps and tatties (turnips and potatoes). We stoked the fire up, and set it on 'slow burning' so that its cheery glow would greet us in the morning. Finally, we flopped into bed and were lulled to sleep by the comforting creaking of the chalet's wooden walls as they trembled in a promising north-easterly, and by the reassurance of our neighbour's words: 'That should bring something.'

Came the Sabbath. The rain had stopped. The wind had dropped. It was grey but perfectly fine. An ideal day for exploring the island. The word 'skerries' is a common name for any little group of rocks throughout the Northern Isles. Out Skerries is rather more than just a couple of rocks, but not that much more. The thing that immediately struck us, as we left the chalet and gazed round, was that we really were surrounded by the sea. The closeness of the coast on every side reminded us just how tiny the island was. Or rather, islands. Actually, there are two. Housay is the larger one. It is elongated, and about two miles from tip to tip. Bruray (or Eastern Isle) is roughly circular, hardly half a mile in diameter. You can cover all the likely bird spots in about three hours, though if you closely followed the indented coastline all the way, it would probably take a full day. Housay and Bruray are joined by a short bridge but, presumably as a legacy of the time when they were separated, each island has its own shop. One was bright and light, and run by cheery lady. It sold mostly essential food items. The other was almost pitch dark inside, and was run by a mysterious bloke who never said a word. It was so dark in there you couldn't actually see what it sold, but we eventually discovered that it stocked just about everything, including luxury items such as cassettes of James Last's greatest hits, and souvenirs that ranged from little model boats to porcelain puppies with 'A Present from Out Skerries' painted on their collars. You could also purchase alcohol from the silent man. Whatever you asked for he seemed to have, but he would never actually say so. Instead, he would always disappear upstairs, come back with a bottle wrapped up in brown paper, and then secrete it under your potatoes. As far as I know, what he was doing wasn't illegal, but maybe he just liked to pretend it was. Perhaps it added a little air of mystery to the routine of island life. Anyway, we didn't discover any of this till later, as both shops were closed on Sunday.

As we wandered round and failed to see a living soul, we realized that everyone was in the kirk for the early-morning service, so we took the opportunity to peer into the yards and gardens of the various dwelling places, to see if there were any birds sheltering behind the walls or in the tiny rhubarb patches which offered cover just about as dense as it gets on Skerries. There are no trees. It didn't take long to check the residential areas, as only about sixty people live on the island, in a variety of buildings, including a row of council houses, a scattering of bungalows, and several traditional grey stone crofts. All these are served by about half a mile of tarmac road, which was, of course, totally traffic free. Until church finished. Then suddenly we had to leap for our lives as at least a dozen vehicles came careering down the hill taking the worshippers back for breakfast. It was a bit alarming to discover that the 'Sunday drivers' syndrome was alive and well on an island where it seemed almost unnecessary to own a car at all. It was even more alarming when a couple of youngsters slipped into 'teenage tearaway' mode and started tazzing around on clapped-out motor bikes, doing 'wheelies' and skid turns. Fortunately, the great thing about a road that is only half a mile long and goes nowhere is that is is very easy to walk away from it. So we did.

For the rest of the morning we explored the rest of the island. I love this process of familiarizing yourself with a new place, trying to anticipate the birds' favourite areas. It is particularly challenging on a typical Northern Isle which, at first glance, looks bleak and birdless, until you discover the hot spots. All islands have them, and Skerries has several. First, we checked the main valley, walking

either side of the wall that runs down its length – no more
than a couple of hundred yards. In Shetland, these walls
replace the hedges. Birds feed along them and even
disappear 'inside' them, hiding amongst the stones just as
they would in foliage. That morning, there were only a
couple of Willow Warblers flitting ahead of us, but it was
enough to give us hope. It was easy to imagine something
rarer. Alongside the wall was the marshy stream.

'Looks good for Bluethroats,' I muttered.

One heard me and hopped out. The first good bird of
the day. Nice one.

The small ploughed fields on one side of the valley
looked like wheatear territory, and there were indeed
several trotting around there. The grassy bank on the other
side had several little stone outcrops that should have
provided ideal Whinchat perches. They did. We scanned
them, and counted half a dozen Whinchats. It didn't feel
like a massive 'fall' but, yes indeed, the nor'easter had
definitely brought something in.

From the main valley we climbed over a slope and found
ourselves gazing down on what looked like some kind of
archaeological site. There was a large hollow in the terrain
– nearly 100 metres across – in which the turf had been
nibbled as neatly as a cricket pitch by the island rabbits. As
we approached, the bunnies took refuge amongst a
network of cairns. The whole area was studded with these
neat piles of stones, and between them there appeared to
be the remains of walls, or maybe foundations. The place
was strangely calm and sheltered from the winds and
would, it struck us, have been completely invisible until
you arrived at it. It was like some kind of lost or hidden
village. We later discovered that this was exactly the case.
This was where the islanders had lived during the era of
the notorious Navy press-gangs who, on sailing past
Skerries in search of recruits, had seen no dwellings and

assumed that it was uninhabited. It was so peaceful in the 'secret valley', as we christened it, that we couldn't help wondering why the village had been deserted in later years. Perhaps because there wasn't much of a view from down there! But there *were* a couple more Bluethroats.

Over the next hillock was another hidden habitat, this time a small freshwater pool with marshy fringes. There were skuas and gulls bathing in the water, a couple of Wood Sandpipers teetering around in the boggy bit, and more Whinchats along the nearby wall. Another spot to keep an eye on. After that, we risked the Sunday drivers and crossed over the bridge to the Eastern Isle, and checked another small pool and several little patches of crops. All the time I kept enthusing to Andrew about how everything was 'scaled down' compared, for example, with Fair Isle. There the crop fields are pretty big, and once a bird scuttles off into the middle it can be amazingly hard to see, even if the spring wheat is barely an inch or two high. On Skerries, a lark or a bunting would have to be wearing camouflaged combat gear to escape detection. We had a reassuring feeling that if there was anything good around we were going to find it. All we had to do was keep going.

But man cannot live on optimism alone. Mid-morning, we popped back to the chalet for a coffee and a biscuit, and to put some more coal on the fire, as we'd been instructed. Adrenalin was keeping us warm enough, but in fact it was pretty nippy, and we wanted to make sure we'd get back to a veritable oven when we'd finished our round. With its steamed-up windows and wooden walls, the place was rapidly becoming probably the most northerly sauna in Britain.

As we set out again, we noticed that the kirkyard car park had filled up for the second service of the day. During the week, most of the men on the island wear chunky Norwegian-style pullovers with bold patterns on them, which makes them look like rather endearing overgrown toddlers in nice woolly pullovers. On Sunday, however, this cosy costume is forsaken in favour of 'Sunday best': austere dark suits and ties for the gents, and smart frocks or coats with gloves and hats for the ladies. Personally, if I were God, I'd prefer being worshipped in a jolly sweater. I don't remember the Bible mentioning anything about having to wear a suit and tie, but I suppose getting dressed up is part of the ritual that helps pass a Sunday on a remote island.

The wheezing of the organ and the fifty-ninth verse of 'For Those in Peril on the Sea' faded on the breeze as we continued on the relatively long walk south-westwards down Housay. It took us through several birdless zones, but also past another little wall-with-stream bit, which I later learnt was where Iain Robertson had found the famous live Ovenbird. The last stop was a sort of mini-ravine, with a sheltered pebbly beach at the bottom of it, which Andrew and I christened 'Mars Bar Gully' because we felt we deserved to stop and have an energy-giving munch after the slightly foot-wearying walk. It also provided us with the excuse just to sit and stare for a while – which in fact turned out to be the appropriate technique for finding birds. It is typical of Shetland birding that you can gaze at an apparently barren cliff face for half an hour, before your eyes suddenly focus on a warbler that has probably been clinging in full view the whole time. I find it incredibly exciting to see these migrants so completely out of context – as on that morning. OK, it was only a Willow Warbler catching flies down there, but it certainly wasn't on willows ... for the moment, it was a Seaweed Warbler. As I dragged out the time it takes to eat a Mars Bar by licking it very slowly like an ice-cream – ever tried it? it looks revolting but tastes terrific! – I sighed with satisfaction at the fact that we'd so completely rescued the holiday after the initial traumas. No more clattering helicopters or chundering oilmen. The only sounds we could hear were the constant chattering of Arctic Terns, the occasional piping of Oystercatchers, and a lot of baaing.

Sheep always sound rather mournful to me. On Skerries, it is not without reason. It must be a lonesome and frustrating predicament, when there's a whole vista of chewable grass all around you, to find yourself tied securely to the end of a short rope. Reason enough to let out the occasional plaintive bleat. I'm not really sure why most of the sheep on Skerries are tethered, but they are. What makes it worse is that they don't seem to realize it. Heaven knows, I don't want to be accused of being sheepist, and I dare say they thoroughly resent being stereotyped as stupid, but ... it doesn't matter how delicately you attempt to tiptoe past one of the dimwitted Skerries sheep, muttering comforting words and trying desperately not to panic them, you can be absolutely certain that, at some point, they will turn and look at you, leap three feet in the air, and then race away as if they've been shot in their woolly bums. Until they reach the end of their tether. At which point, the rope will yank them back, nearly pulling their heads off, and leaving them splayed out like a rug. And it doesn't matter how many times you walk past the same sheep reassuring them and reminding them – 'don't panic, and don't forget you're on a rope' – they *never* learn. The only variation is provided by the ones that run round and round in circles going so fast that their feet leave the ground and they momentarily do a flying circuit before panicking and plummeting. I can't pretend it isn't entertaining, but it is rather dumb. Mind you ... I'm criticizing the sheep, but I couldn't help wondering about one of the islanders who had tethered his animal close to the edge of a cliff, without first measuring the length of the rope. We heard the bleating, and then it went ominously quiet, and then we saw it, pathetically dangling where it had tumbled over the edge and accidentally hanged itself. Or maybe it had decided to 'end it all'. Better that than the mint sauce.

Anyway – enough of sheep, back to the birds. By the end of the morning, we had sort of 'mapped out' the likely Skerries hot spots. Since that first day, I have returned to the island many times, and I inevitably associate each area with birds I have seen there. Over the years there have been some good ones. Pallas's Grasshopper Warbler along the valley wall, Black-eared Wheatear in the main field, Lesser Grey Shrike in the secret valley, Rustic Bunting in Mars Bar Gully, and many many more. Meanwhile, back on 11 May 1975, Andrew and I made our way back to the chalet for a well-earned lunch, adding up our morning total and feeling pretty satisfied: thirty-five Wheatears, ten Whinchats, two Redstarts, two Black Redstarts, three Willow Warblers, two Chiffchaffs, and no fewer than eight Bluethroats. If you've never seen a Bluethroat, or have maybe just managed to tick off a skulky autumn juvenile, let me assure you that a full-plumaged spring male is something well worth travelling for. From behind, they look like a slightly overgrown Robin, but when they turn round it is as if they are wearing a luminous Union Jack waistcoat. One Bluethroat is pretty satisfying; eight gave us a *very* warm glow. But it was about to get warmer.

We plodded back into a now freshening wind, looking forward to toasting our tootsies in front of the fire in our cosy little cabin. As I came over the hill, I could see smoke curling up from our chimney. Then suddenly the curl became more of a billow. For a moment, I panicked. Then I came to the conclusion that someone must have been burning something behind the hut, thus creating a rather disturbing illusion. I sighed with relief as I pointed it out to

Andrew, who was slightly behind me.

'Look at that,' I said. 'It looks like the chalet's on fire.'

Then we realized. It was.

The outbreak of the blaze had coincided nicely with turning-out time at the nearby church, thus giving a whole new meaning to 'hell-fire' preaching. We raced over the horizon to discover a line of island men in their Sunday best efficiently passing buckets of water from the nearest house and emptying them over the outside of the chalet. This wasn't actually terribly effective, as the fire was smouldering away inside. So was most of our gear. It was immediately clear that the men had no intention of singeing their nice suits, so Andrew and I donned protective clothing, in the form of a couple of sets of bright yellow oilskins, and hurled ourselves in and out of the inferno rescuing what we could. Every time we came out, the islanders threw buckets of freezing cold water over us. They later claimed that they kept mistaking us for flames. A likely story, made all the less credible by the fact that everyone was falling about laughing. Except us who, between getting alternately smoked and soaked, were becoming rapidly convinced that this was now turning into the holiday from hell.

By mid-afternoon, the fire was out. Fortunately, the bedroom doors had been shut and, and though most of our clothes looked as if they had been charcoal-grilled, not much had been totally ruined. Except, unfortunately, Andrew's binoculars which, ironically, he had left in the hearth to 'demist' after our previous day's drenching on the boat. They'd certainly dried out. Alas, they'd also split in two. The main room of the chalet had been totally gutted. The place was completely ruined.

It wasn't the easiest phone call I've ever had to make.

'Er ... hallo, is that Mr Johnson?'

'Yes.'

'Well, er … it's Bill Oddie here. You very kindly arranged with Dr Marshall that we could stay in your holiday home on Skerries.'

'Oh aye.'

'Well … we've burnt it down!'

Mr Johnson seemed so unperturbed that, for a moment, I could have sworn he said 'thank you'. What he did say was, 'Oh, never mind.'

As I put the phone down, I almost felt as if he'd been expecting it. It seems the other islanders certainly had. 'That wall behind the fire got awful hot. We didn't think it was properly insulated. We thought that was going to happen some day.'

Andy and I couldn't help wondering why, then, had they told us to keep putting coal on the fire, and why hadn't they warned us? But then we thought we probably knew the answer. The fire had been the best fun they'd had on the island for years! And involving a TV star, no less. A guaranteed front-page story for the *Shetland Times* – they were probably developing the photos at that very minute. There was no harm done, and the place was no doubt heavily insured. So the locals were happy, and so too was Mr Johnson. But we certainly weren't.

Yet again, I was overcome by a not entirely illogical feeling that the trip was utterly cursed. It had been going rather well that morning but, believe me, there's nothing like burning down somebody's holiday retreat to take the edge off a good day's bird-watching. This time I really did think we should pack it in as a bad job, and go home. But the Skerries folk wouldn't hear of it. Probably out of gratitude for entertaining them so richly, they inundated us with offers of accommodation. We chose to move into a cosy little house overlooking the main valley, complete with lovely big soft beds, a telly, delicious home cooking, and even a spare pair of binoculars for Andy to borrow.

Suddenly, things didn't seem so bad after all.

And yet this bizarrely memorable trip still had one final trick to turn. It was as if someone up there was testing our resilience by exposing us to extremes. Most of the next day was spent ambling round the island, repeatedly trying to convince ourselves that the fire hadn't been our fault. By late afternoon, we'd just about succeeded. We decided to get on with the bird-watching, only to realize that there were no longer very many birds to watch. That morning, there had still been a reasonably variety of migrants on the island, including four of the Bluethroats, but on our final round we couldn't find any. The following morning was even more birdless, and it was drizzling. Ominously, it was the 13th: unlucky or totally useless? By midday the howling wind had returned, and it was raining so hard that bird-watching was impossible. At least we were now installed in a snug waterproof stone house in which we could build the fire up as hot as we liked. Even so, it seemed pointless being awake. After lunch, we both retired for an afternoon nap. Once more, my depression took over. I huddled under the eiderdown, remembering the optimism when we'd planned this trip. The conviction that we were going to try 'something different'. Then I thought of how it had turned out. I tried to summon up the Bartley spirit: 'When it hurts, it's doing you good.' But it was no consolation. It didn't feel too good to me. I fell asleep, convinced that we'd been 'hard done-by'. It wasn't fair. We really did deserve something better than this. We got it.

Jessie, the lady of the house, woke us up by gently tapping on the door.

'There's a wee black-and-white bird sitting on my washing-line. I don't know if it's anything but...'

The number of times a bird-watcher is summoned by a non-birder to see a 'funny bird', and it actually turns out to be something worth seeing, can be numbered on the fingers of a mittened hand, but there was no way we would have hurt Jessie's feelings by turning over and going back to sleep, which is probably what we really wanted to do. We got up, and followed her into the kitchen.

'It could be a Pied Flycatcher,' we suggested, trying to sound enthusiastic. At least that would be a 'trip tick'. 'Unless, of course, it's a...'

We were about to leap into the realms of fantasy, when the fantasy flitted into view. There, perched between the clothes pegs, hardly a metre from the window, was an exquisite male Collared Flycatcher. (At the time the fifth British record.)

That evening, in a final act of poetic justice, Brian Marshall was able to come over from Whalsay and join us enjoying the bird as it posed on an old fence down by the shoreline, against a calm clear sea, under a blue sky, on a beautiful sunny Shetland evening. It was an image I shall never forget. A bird-watching magic moment.

Some you win ... eventually.

PS: Things have changed quite a bit up in Shetland since those good (!?) old days. In fact, the oil effect has abated, at least to the extent that the construction work has long been completed, and the air traffic is not so frantic. Sumburgh Airport is highly efficient, and so too is the system of inter-island travel, using small planes or extremely stable – and dry – ferries. There is also a much larger number of birders living on and visiting the islands, and an extremely comprehensive information network. This has not only confirmed the theory that rare birds do indeed turn up all over the islands, but has also greatly increased the chances of seeing them. Accommodation is excellent, at a variety of prices, and the scenery is as wild and wonderful as ever. And if this sounds like a travel commercial, it is.

6
'Well, If This is NEW Guinea …'
Papua New Guinea

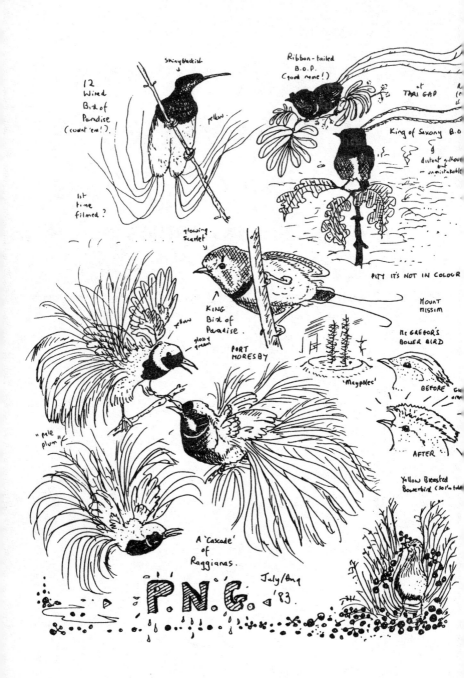

12 Wired Bird of Paradise (count 'em!)!

Shinyblackish

yellow

1st time filmed?

Ribbon-tailed B.O.P. (good name!)

at TARI GAP

King of Saxony B.O.

distant silhouette but unmistakable

glowing scarlet

KING Bird of Paradise.

glow

glossy green

PORT MORESBY

"pale plum"

PITY IT'S NOT IN COLOUR

MOUNT MISSIM

Mc GREGOR'S BOWER BIRD

'Maypoles'

BEFORE

AFTER

Yellow Breasted Bowerbird (sort of told)

A 'Cascade' of Raggianas.

P.N.G.

July/Aug '83

PNG. It sounds like some kind of 'woman's complaint'. Well, indeed it was. In fact, the woman was called Laura. She and I had been going out – and indeed living together – for quite a few years until, some time in the spring of 1983, I 'popped the question'. In fact, I popped two questions. I asked her if she'd care to get married, and if she'd like to spend our honeymoon in Papua New Guinea. That's what PNG stands for: Papua New Guinea. In retrospect, it could also stand for 'Post-Nuptial Grumps'. But it wasn't just Laura's complaint. I suffered from it too. And all I can say is I'm glad it doesn't happen every month!

In fact, it was the BBC's idea. Some time in April 1983 a producer from the Natural History Unit – I shall call him Richard, 'cos that's his name – rang me and asked if I fancied doing a sort of ornithological mini-series in PNG. It would involve three weeks' filming in late July. This just happened to be the month Laura and I had chosen for our wedding. July tends to have nice weather, and it's also the month I was born in, so we could have a combined wedding and birthday party and save a bit of money on the catering. Now, talking of saving money, here was another chance. I was immediately taken by the idea of the BBC footing the bill for the honeymoon, so I negotiated with them that, instead of paying me a fee, they'd provide an extra ticket so Laura could join me on the trip. Of course, I'm doing myself down. I'm not really such a total skinflint. The truth was that I couldn't bear leaving my new wife two days after the wedding night. I simply wouldn't have gone without her. Mind you, I think I had another, rather perverse, motive. I had a feeling that the trip was going to be something of an experience (euphemism for 'living hell') and it would sort of ... test the marriage. This was something I may subconsciously have been anxious to do, since this was my second, and if it wasn't going to last I'd rather know as soon as possible so I could finally give up on relationships and become a hermit or a monk, or something equally celibate: a twitcher, perhaps. Well, just in case you're wondering, it's now over ten years later and Laura and I are still very happily married. Isn't that heart-warming? Mind you, it was no thanks to PNG. So ... back to 1983.

What did we know about Papua New Guinea? Well, we'd seen it on telly. Most of us have, if only in ancient scratchy black-and-white film of explorers discovering lost tribes who, in turn, are encountering their first white men. You know the bit, where the commentator says: 'Until this moment these primitive tribesmen had never actually seen a white man.' Mmm ... well, I always wonder about that. How could the famous explorer really be the first white man, when the chances are that a whole film crew turned up first to negotiate with the lost tribe, figure out the best camera angles, sort out make-up and costumes for a photogenic tribal dance, and probably negotiate repeat fees? I reckon, that if the truth were known, the first white person these tribes actually saw was a researcher from the BBC. And, come to think of it, how do we really know that they hadn't seen any white men before? Do we just take their word for it? Well, come on ... these tribes may have been 'lost', but they weren't stupid. Faced with the opportunity of appearing on the telly, they're hardly going to blow their chances, are they? 'Now, before we start filming,' says the researcher, 'I have to ask you to sign this contract saying you've never seen a white man before.'

Well, be honest, they're not going to own up: 'Oh, well, the fact is ... we had *Survival* here last month; *National Geographic* at the weekend; and *The Really Wild Show* are due in next week!' No, they're just going to shake their heads, and point and panic when the plane comes in, and mime stuff about 'great iron birds', just like they're expected to.

But I digress. I'm being silly, aren't I? Well, not *that* silly. I'd really like to make a point here about television travelogues. The fact is that there aren't many places in the world where television hasn't reached. There can't be many genuinely lost tribes that aren't wily in the ways of film-makers. Moreover we, the viewers, have become positively blasé about seeing faraway places and strange-looking people 'on the box'. This familiarity can have a strange and possibly worrying effect on a traveller. I really do believe there is a syndrome these days by which, because we have seen just about everything and everywhere on the telly, when we actually do visit these countries it's almost as if it's not real. It's like if you go on safari to Kenya. Are these genuine Masai tribesmen or are they extras on a film set? Even the animals are suspect. Are they trained, or animatronics, or even two fellas in a lion skin? Oops. Being silly again.

So what is this serious point I'm trying to make? What I'm saying is ... there is danger here. Explorers and great white hunters always warned that we must respect the wild or risk the consequences. It wasn't difficult years ago. Unfamiliarity breeds fear. If you'd never been in a jungle or heard the cries of wild animals, such things were indeed very scary when you first experienced them. But it's not quite the same these days, when the rain forest is as familiar a telly image as the *Blue Peter* garden. I mean no disrespect to *Blue Peter* but I'm not scared of it (though I did used to be scared of its formidable woman producer).

What's more, I have wandered through a jungle and felt equally unperturbed. And that is worrying. And very unwise. So the point I'm making is that, just because we've seen these faraway places in wildlife documentaries, doesn't mean that they are safe, and travellers would do well to keep reminding themselves of that. Which brings me back to PNG.

Where was I? Oh yes, PNG facts. It's a long way away. Right over the other side of the world, just above Australia. In fact, New Guinea is a great big island divided into two. The western half is Irian Jaya and the eastern half PNG. In 1983 Irian Jaya was seriously wild and dangerous, and it was not easy or wise to visit it. There were certainly still cannibals and head-hunters living there. In PNG there weren't any cannibals or head-hunters any more – well, probably not. There were definitely still large areas of almost unexplored jungle, so there *might* have been been cannibals and head-hunters hidden in them. There was certainly lots of exotic wildlife, including enormous insects and, most notably, birds of paradise. So our honeymoon would involve flying to the other side of the world to film in the jungle. Now at this point, I'm sure Laura would wish me to point out – sympathetically – that, back in the early eighties, she had a few phobias. Nothing to be embarrassed about; in fact, she shared them with a large percentage of the human race. She did not care much for spiders and other creepy-crawlies; she was not happy being driven at breakneck speed; and she was somewhat nervous of flying. Neither was she too keen on being cooked or beheaded. On the plus side, she had nothing against birds of paradise though, all in all, she probably wouldn't have chosen PNG as her ideal honeymoon destination had she known what it entailed. But she didn't. So off we went.

It didn't start well. The taxi was late and attempted to

take the scenic route from north London to Gatwick Airport, which is difficult 'cos there isn't one. The driver suddenly realized we were going to miss the plane and began tazzing and swerving down the M23 as if he was in a car chase from a James Bond movie. Phobia number one faced already. At least it brought us closer together: clinging to one another in the back seat. We caught the plane with minutes to spare but remained nervous wrecks all the way to our first stopover at Colombo in Sri Lanka. There we realized that the car journey hadn't been so bad after all, as we learnt the meaning of *real* fear. Sri Lanka was in the middle of some kind of military coup! It was rumoured that guerrillas might attempt to take the airport at any time. We cowered in the transit lounge for four hours with the sound of bombs and gunfire echoing in the distance. Fortunately, it never got any closer. We took off again, suffered no greater trauma at Singapore than being ripped off at the duty-free shop, and finally landed at Port Moresby, the capital of PNG.

The whole journey had actually taken little more that twenty-four hours. One day. You can take as long to get across London after a rainstorm. One day. There we were in a very foreign country. And yet the hotel resembled any other Holiday Inn lookalike. A kettle and coffee in the room, along with a courtesy bar, a mint on the pillow, and twin beds. It wasn't exactly the bridal suite, but Laura was content enough. She settled down by the swimming-pool with an iced drink in one hand and a good book in the other. One day. Were we really in New Guinea? Were there really tribesmen and birds of paradise out there? I set off to find out.

The first stage of any on-location wildlife or travel filming trip is a planning meeting. This involves meeting 'the crew' (who've probably flown in from some other assignment) and discussing 'the concept'. Our crew was small in number, but big on experience. They were a pair of American brothers, Neil and Joel Rettig (avid watchers of credits on wildlife spectaculars may have clocked their names). Neil is the cameraman and Joel the sound man. They had just flown in from somewhere in South America, where they had spent months enduring tropical diseases and poisonous plants to capture twenty seconds of something for the latest David Attenborough blockbuster. PNG with Bill Oddie must have been a bit of a comedown for them! Or maybe they expected it to be light relief. They'd find out! The other 'crew' members at the meeting were Richard (the producer/director) and Beth, his production assistant. The PA on a shoot like this really does have the toughest job of all. She (or, rarely, he) is responsible for the logistics of the whole operation. This means everything from making travel arrangements (in countries where phones may not work or planes may not fly) to typing up the ever-changing daily schedules, to searching for diarrhoea tablets for ailing presenters (i.e. me). The PA does a lot else besides, but I've never really dared ask what, 'cos I know I'd feel eternally guilty that *my* job is so comparatively easy. All I have to do is follow 'the concept' and make it sound interesting, and if I couldn't make PNG interesting, then I was surely in the wrong job. To help us figure out exactly what we were going to film we had a local 'fixer', who just happened also to be a wildlife expert, and a bird-watcher in particular. He also happened to be English.

This is a universal syndrome. Wherever I have been birding or filming across the world, whether it be PNG, Hong Kong or the Galapagos, there has always been an expatriate Briton who is revered as the local expert, even by the locals! I really don't want to get all patriotic about this, but one of the few claims the British can still have to being deserving of international respect is that we produce brilliant bird-watchers. I will say no more, except to revel in the reflected expertise of the then PNG representative of this distinguished breed: Brian Finch (he'd even got the name for it). In fact, when I was introduced to Brian in Port Moresby, his face seemed vaguely familiar. As it turned out, it probably was. We reckoned that we had both been present at a twitch (we thought probably in the Scilly Isles), so we may well have subliminally registered one another in between gasping at the glory of some little brown warbler. Brian had been a Sussex regular (and therefore we also shared a few mutual acquaintances) before moving to PNG. I think he had a 'proper job' at the local shipping company, but he was clearly really there for the birds. He already knew them very well indeed. He also knew the local language, and could advise us on logistics (that word again) and potential problems. Brian was obviously the man to consult about 'the concept'.

Richard's overall idea was that he wanted to film PNG through the eyes of a British birder who had no experience whatsoever of the conditions or species that he would encounter. That was my role. Good casting. I liked this approach, because it would be shot in 'real time' (not over several months, as most wildlife programmes have to be), and I hoped we could include stuff about the practical problems of bird-watching that I felt had never really been covered on television. (And I still feel that, over ten years later!) I was asked what would my first quest be when I landed in a foreign land?

'Find the local sewage farm,' I replied.

Richard was a little taken aback by this answer, but Brian knew exactly what I meant. Heaven knows, I could write reams on 'great sewage farms I have known', from happy teenage days when Perry Oaks (by Heathrow Airport) was still open to the public, to the almost legendary Werribee (Melbourne, Australia), which has more waterbirds than the Okavango (Botswana). I'm sure any birder will confirm that the smell of festering sewage is as seductive as an exotic aftershave when it comes to attracting the birds (I suspect there's some slightly sexist pun in there somewhere. Sorry). Moreover, there is something comforting about a sewage farm as your first stop in a faraway land. It's nothing to do with going back to nature. It's just that waders (which *love* sewage) are just about the most ubiquitous group of birds – some species occur just about all around the globe – and it's not quite such an ornithological culture shock to be greeted by Common Sandpipers, Turnstones or Greenshanks, rather than some weird little jungle-dweller, with an unpronounceable name, which you can't even ascribe to a familiar family. What's more, seeing these old friends always reminds me of the amazing journeys that birds are capable of, which I find the single most exciting aspect of bird study: the wonder of migration. So, you see, for me, a visit to a sewage farm is almost a spiritual experience! As it happens, and as Brian informed us, Port Moresby was a beauty! More of that anon.

Meanwhile, Richard was also anxious to be sure that we would be able to track down and film some birds of paradise. No problem, Brian assured him. Also, we wanted to find a genuine New Guinea tribesman; well, Richard did – I wasn't quite so sure. It was, however, a crucial part of Richard's concept, as I would soon discover. Again, no problem. Brian would fix us up with a 'local', as they were colloquially known. And talking of euphemisms ... Brian also warned us to beware of 'rascals'. He smiled as he used the word, but I could tell he was worryingly serious. I'd also noticed that the door to his flat had a double mortise lock and several security chains on it. OK, so what are 'rascals'? we asked. They didn't sound too fearsome in a land that could boast cannibals and head-hunters. In fact, they were (and still are) far more troublesome. Whether the escalating crime rate in PNG was (and still is) the result of 'western ways' (drink, drugs, and plenty of stealable goods) I wouldn't like to conjecture (though no doubt it is), but the fact was, Brian warned us, we really ought to be alert and careful. 'Don't leave valuables around, don't leave cars unlocked, don't let women walk out on their own, indeed be careful where you go on your own, etc. etc. etc.'

No, this wasn't downtown Los Angeles. This was Port Moresby, Papua New Guinea. 'Probably you'll be fine,' Brian assured us cheerfully, 'but just be careful. OK?' Well, yeah. OK. But own up, we are talking dangerous criminals here, aren't we? 'Rascals!' Come on! It's a bit like calling serial killers 'Scamps'!

On our first *après*-jet-lag afternoon we were filming our first local. There we were, our little crew: Neil crouched over his camera, Joel fiddling with his tape recorder, Beth jotting down continuity notes, Richard directing, and me interviewing the biggest tribal chieftain you ever did see. He really was an impressive fellow, with a physique that belonged in the second row of an All Blacks scrum. And fierce-looking with it, though wondrously photogenic. A grass 'skirt' (would they be narked if they knew we called them 'skirts'?), body paint, a spear, and an absolutely enormous feather head-dress that would not have looked out of place on a showgirl at the Folies Bergère or on Mrs Shilling at Ascot. Richard's concept was that the film would start with Brian pointing out to me the various feathers on the chief's head-dress, and explaining which birds they had come from. My quest would then be to go and try and see the birds alive in the jungle, 'where they belonged'. I took Richard aside and whispered my slight concern that the chief might take this approach as some sort of veiled insult – like I was saying that feathers look better on birds that stuck on blokes' heads. Richard took my point, and it was agreed that I could add that bit later in 'voice-over'. For the moment, Brian would simply identify the feathers, and I would express great admiration of the Chief's lovely hat and leave it at that.

So it was. It did seem as if the head-dress contained a fair cross-section of New Guinea avifauna and other wildlife trophies. Along the top was a huge fan of red feathers plucked from the rumps of a (now-defunct?) colony of parakeets. Stretching from ear to ear was a strange elongated serrated feather that had formerly adorned the crown of the extremely rare King of Saxony Bird of Paradise, and through the Chief's nose was a slim bone from some bit of a wild boar. The whole effect was undeniably dazzling. Until the camera went in for the close-ups. In fact, the boar's bone turned out to be a cocktail stick. The King of Saxony feather had been carefully cut out of a strip of cardboard, and the parakeet tails (though real) had been stuck in with chewing gum! It seemed more than likely that he'd learnt how to put it all together by watching videos of *Blue Peter*! The truth was that 'the Chief' dressed up like this every Saturday morning and stood by the main road into Port Moresby posing for tourists and any passing film crews. The rest of the week, he was a bank manager. Presumably *not* dressed up like that (though it did strike me that if he was, I might well switch my account immediately). Moreover, being a bank manager, he was more than astute in matters of finance, as Richard discovered when another 'local' – this time in the more typical costume of denim shorts and Hawaiian shirt – popped out of the bushes to sort out the fee. He turned out to be the bank manager's agent, no less! To be honest, I had to laugh. And I think the viewers would have done too, if I'd have been allowed to tell them. But I wasn't.

It's a difficult decision that wildlife-film makers have to make: do you own up about the stuff that goes on 'behind the cameras', or not? I think most viewers are pretty much aware that all may not be exactly as it seems, and that a finished film may well involve a certain amount of 'fixing' and judicious editing ('cheating', it has been called, rather unfairly). Personally, I find it all rather fascinating and I confess to often being more intrigued by the 'making' of documentaries than by the finished articles, in which nature often seems to be out there in some sort of wonderful unspoilt vacuum. But then again, there's a case for establishing a mood and sticking with it, and I must admit that if you start off a series by admitting that the native chief is really a bank manager you do lessen the magic a bit! Anyway, at the time it was my first experience of this kind of 'shall-we-own-up-or-not?' type of decision. It was not to be the last.

Next day, I offered Laura the sort of honeymoon treat every new bride must surely dream of: a trip to a sewage farm. I realized I'd married the right woman when she accepted. That's my kinda gal. As it happens, I think I can probably thank Brian for enticing her along. Not only was he witty and entertaining company, but he should have been a sewage salesman. By the time he'd finished extolling the virtues of what he poetically referred to as the 'shit pit', he'd made it sound as delightful as Kew Gardens. The amazing thing was that he was right. The Port Moresby shit pit had manicured lawns, walkways shaded by blossom-filled trees, in turn filled with Rainbow Bee-eaters, and, of course, expansive lagoons filled with ... birds. There were herons and egrets, waders and waterfowl, gulls and terns. All incredibly easy to film, and especially spectacular when they took to the air as a Whistling Kite soared over and panicked them. Neil filmed the sights. Joel recorded the sounds. Richard was delighted, and I was forgotten. So was my contribution to 'the concept'. Ironically, footage of actual wildlife is invariably the most difficult thing to get. It's easy to film me rabbiting on to the camera, but not so easy to fill the frame with wildfowl, as they did that afternoon. As it turned out, they never really got anything to match it during the next three weeks. The result was that whenever pictures of good-looking birds were required, they cut in stuff from the sewage farm and made it match whatever wetland we happened to be at. I can't blame 'em, but my eulogy extolling the shit pit was left on the cutting-room floor. I was a bit sad. I'd rather set my heart on being the first wildlife presenter to use the 'S-word' on telly! Never mind, at least I had a consolation. Whilst we were there, Brian located a mega-rarity. A first for New Guinea: a Starling!

Richard wasn't very interested in filming the Starling. What he wanted now was birds of paradise. So did I. We discussed the matter with Brian. We presumed that we would have to hack our way deep into the jungle to dig out these almost legendary avian jewels. Not a bit of it. Half an hour after asking, we were driving along the main road out of Port Moresby. We went past a bunch of rascals playfully smashing in a shop window, past the bank manager now doing a war-dance for a Japanese film crew, took a couple of turnings, drove up a bit of a hill, and swung off into what looked like a pretty well-used car park. Hardly had we tumbled out of the car than we heard a sound that instantly reminded me of David Attenborough. No, not an accountant gasping at the size of his budgets. This was a sort of massed whooping noise. Had I not known better I think I would have assumed it was coming from a team of excited monkeys. But I *did* know better. I'd heard this on the telly, and as I listened I could also hear Mr Attenborough whispering in my head: 'This is the sound of the Raggiana Bird of Paradise.' And indeed it was. Only it wasn't just one. There, leaping around up in the tree-tops, was a whole bunch of them. Only 'bunch' can't possibly be the collective name for birds of paradise, can it? 'Flock'? No. How about a 'cascade'? They *were* cascading, but they were also bouncing and bobbing and flapping, and even dangling. It was a mass display: several males showing off to a couple of females. And they certainly had something to show off. The male's basic body size isn't much more than that of a European Blackbird, but when it fluffs up all its feathers it looks as big as a chicken. But a lot prettier! How can one put it down on paper? I mean, really I advise you to look 'em up in a PNG field guide or, better still, find some of John Gould's wonderful engravings, or get a video, or go to New Guinea ... But, just for the record: the Raggiana has a yellow head and mantle; an iridescent green face, with an ivory-white bill; a shiny purple breast-plate; maroon underparts; and red or orange flank plumes. And it's those flank plumes that really 'blow your mind' (I think an old hippy phrase is quite appropriate, 'cos the bird does look positively psychedelic!). At first glance, you'd think the plumes were a long dangly tail. But they're not. But who cares what they are? It's what the bird does with them that matters. What it does is ... tip over on a branch, hang almost upside-down, fluff up its plumes like a huge pink powder-puff, and then it trembles all over. Hopefully the females tremble as well. I certainly did. A whole 'cascade' of Raggiana males leaping, dangling and trembling, and whooping is — as I hope you can imagine — a totally unforgettable experience. The only flaw is that they do all this right up at the very top of very tall trees, so by the time you've marvelled at it for half an hour you've got terrible neck ache. It was a pain I was to get very used to by the end of three weeks' rain-forest watching. But it was worth it.

As Brian led me back to the car, attempting to

manipulate my head back into the horizontal plane, I asked him for more info on the birds. What *was* a group of displaying males really called? Apparently, a 'clan'. Mmm ... they didn't *look* Scottish. I preferred 'cascade'. And why were they called Raggiana Birds of Paradise? Surely not 'cos they were sort of 'raggy'? – that would have been an insult. No, the answer was that they were given their name by whoever discovered them. So was that Mr Raggiana then? No, in this case, Raggiana referred to a Count Raggi, who had probably financed the explorer's expedition, and so the bird had been named after him as a 'thank you'. This was a common practice with the birds of paradise and other New Guinea exotics. People were understandably dazzled by them, and so it became quite a compliment to have one named after you. It must have been a good way of raising sponsorship (or patronage, as it was known then). The explorer goes to the rich person and says: 'Pay for the trip and I promise you'll have your very own bird of paradise.' It obviously appealed to the royalty of the day. Not only is there Count Raggi's Bird of Paradise, but also the King of Saxony's, and the Emperor of Germany's, and Queen Carola's, and Princess Stephania's. In the case of the ladies, the compliment may well have been romantically intended. What more likely to endear you to whatever regal lass you fancied than naming a gorgeous bird after her? Can't you just see the Valentine card: 'A cracking bird for a cracking bird!' Oh, those old explorers know how to impress a gal.

I must confess, writing this now has set me thinking. Why doesn't this sort of bird-naming still go on? I know there aren't many (if any) new ones to be discovered, but there's been an awful lot of fuss about 'standardizing' bird names lately, so that they are called the same thing right across the world. For example, we in Britain talk about Lapland Buntings, whilst in America they call them

Lapland Longspurs. So which is it to be? Neither, I say. Personally, I think it's dead boring if birds are called the same thing all over the place. What's more, are we not missing a great opportunity here to raise a bit of much-needed cash for conservation projects? What I suggest is that we 'sell off' each species to the highest bidder, which is essentially what they did back in the old days with the birds of paradise. Naturally, we'd target the people who really do have money. This would, of course, include royalty, who certainly have plenty to spare. So how about Queen Elizabeth's Bunting? Or she'd probably prefer Liz's Longspur, as it has a horsy connotation. Philanthropically inclined businessmen would certainly want a piece of the action: we could have Richard Branson's Pipit (instead of Blyth's Pipit, I'd suggest, Blyth being no more than a deceased ornithologist, long past contributing to the cause), or Maxwell's Murrelet (it's still not too late to improve his image). And if rich folks wanted to flatter their wives or girlfriends, by all means let them buy them a bird. It doesn't have to be a bird of paradise. Anything pretty will do. You could sell off the common ones quite cheaply, so that normal people don't feel left out: Sharon's Tit has a nice feel to it, don't you think? What's more, I think birds should only retain their names for one year, so everyone gets a chance. So, every January, there'd be a big 'auction' when everything changes. I reckon everyone would benefit. There'd be more money for conserving the birds, more fun for the bird-watchers as they try to tick off every species on their life-lists under its new name, *and* – best of all – it would put an end to all these tedious debates about bird names once and for all. If scientists want universal names *use the latin*! (Isn't that what Latin names are for?)

Anyway, *Paradisaea raggiana* was 'in the can' (as we film makers say), and it was time for us to leave Port

Moresby and explore more of PNG. Remember how I said seeing faraway places on television can make them seem disconcertingly over-familiar when you actually go there? Well, the effect is doubled when everything is viewed through the windscreen of a small van. Australians will frequently describe something as 'unreal'. It is often a rather over-used compliment, as 'awesome' has become over the past year or two. Personally, I think 'awesome' is more appropriate to the Grand Canyon than to the latest episode of *Neighbours*. Similarly, I've heard 'unreal' applied to the rush-hour traffic jam in Sydney (which is, as it happens, extremely real). Nevertheless, 'unreal' was exactly the word I felt like applying to my through-the-window view of New Guinea as we got further way from town. And it was unreal in both senses. Wandering along the roadside and peering from the jungle were people dressed in either virtually nothing at all, or all manner of what looked like war-paint or tribal costume. They couldn't *all* be bank managers. And they definitely weren't extras of a film set. From within the 'safety' of our vehicle, it was unreal in the true sense, almost as if we were just watching a travel documentary.

If we stopped to refuel or buy food it became unreal in the 'Australian' sense. It was undeniably weird, and more than a little disturbing. For Heaven's sake, less than a week ago, we'd been mingling with the shoppers in Oxford Street. Now we were being stared at and jostled by people who just might be cannibals or head-hunters and, even if they weren't, you certainly couldn't tell by looking at them! They looked fierce enough, I can tell you. Either that, or they looked funny. Now I'm perfectly aware that it may seem appallingly politically incorrect (or even verging on the racist) to say that, surrounded by these people, we didn't know whether to scream or laugh. But then weren't these exactly the same emotional reactions that were probably going through the minds of the locals as they looked at us? Anyone who has travelled in India or Africa will surely confirm that the local people tend to stare at white visitors with nervousness (which, because it is silent, is easily mistaken for hostility), or else they point and laugh at us (and who can blame them!). All these emotions are born of unfamiliarity: nervousness, suspicion, curiosity, it's all in there. Which really only goes to show that we are all just human, whether we're a New Guinea tribesman or a BBC film crew! Actually, the truth is that *they* were probably more familiar with film crews than *we* were with tribesmen. Indeed, though many did gather round us, many also totally ignored us. But we couldn't take our eyes off *them*. This was culture shock indeed, even if it was purely visual. So did we scream or laugh? We felt that it was probably wise to do neither. We got back in the vehicle and took photos, on a long lens.

In fact, the mixture of 'costume' – dress or undress – was pretty bizarre. At least, it was to us. The truth is, of course, that it was perfectly natural and indeed practical. The climate in PNG is typically tropical, which means hot and wet. The basic national dress is perfectly suited to those conditions: a grass skirt and an umbrella! The same poet who named the sewage farm the 'shit pit' had turned his talents to the grass skirt. It is known locally as 'arse grass' (from which we may perhaps deduce that the poet did not speak with a northern British accent, otherwise it wouldn't rhyme. It works very nicely in southern British, or American, or Australian ... Pause, while you try it). 'Arse grass' is all some of the locals wear. Very practical. It's nice and cool and, when it rains, there's not much to get wet. But why, you may well wonder, bother with the umbrella? Well, think about it. Skin may dry out pretty quickly when the sun appears, but vegetation takes a lot longer. It would be very uncomfortable sitting on soggy arse grass. Hence the brolly. It's a pretty good rule when travelling in exotic lands that 'locals know best'. The visitor really should wear what they wear. But alas, I just couldn't bring myself to do it. I'd look stupid with an umbrella.

Not every local had the minimalist approach to dress. Western influences were obvious. But old habits die hard, and even those kitted out in the standard gear of denim shorts, T-shirts and trainers couldn't resist a touch of the traditional. It was clear that, however mundane the rest of their gear, PNG blokes loved wearing things on their heads. Not everyone had something as spectacular as the roadside bank manager. If they had, there wouldn't have been an unplucked bird left in the country. Indeed, the taking of feathers for 'ceremonial' head-dresses was widely discouraged, and we saw very few. The ones we did see were of very modest proportions, and may well have involved chickens rather than birds of paradise. But this didn't stop the fellas going in for fancy headgear. Moreover, it was obvious why they did it: they thought it was great fun. What's more, they were witty with it. I'll never forget one little gaggle of otherwise intimidatingly butch-looking blokes comparing 'hats'. One had a miner's helmet decorated with bottle-tops and sweet-papers, another wore a corn-flake packet, and the undisputed winner sported a simply enormous curly blond wig that Dolly Parton would have killed for. They pointed at one another and laughed their heads off! And I really don't think they'd have minded if we had done so too. But we didn't risk it.

You see, in a foreign land the most innocent things *can* be misconstrued. Take, for example, pigs. In PNG pigs are money. Not literally, of course. You don't actually go round with a purseful of pigs. Like, if you want to make a phone call, you don't pop into the corner shop and say:

'I'm sorry, I've only got a sow, I wonder could you change it for half a dozen piglets?' Added to which, it'd be cruel to push a piglet into a slot machine.

No, but seriously though – and I do mean seriously – in PNG pigs represent wealth. The more pigs a person owns, the better off they are. Which makes it all the more bizarre that they allow their pigs to run around all over the place. Unless of course it's the New Guinea equivalent of 'flashing it about: Look, I'm so well off I let my pigs go scampering around on the main road.'

Well, therein lies the danger. As you are driving along there are indeed pigs and piglets running, ambling or even sleeping, in the middle of the road. They are hard to avoid. But you must, at all costs, because if you run over a pig you are in serious trouble. At worst, the pig owner may literally demand your execution. Yes, that's right – people have actually been killed because they ran over a pig. One can't help thinking that the pig owner must have been looking for an excuse for bloodshed since he was making no attempt to curb his pig's suicidal tendencies by allowing it to wander around on the highway, but apparently that doesn't matter. Pigs are so sacrosanct that they can roam where they like, and the fact is that in PNG the loss of a pig could be a motive for murder. Probably it rarely goes that far, but you must still not run over a pig because, at the very least, you will be liable to 'payback'.

'Payback' is a principle that is at the very core of PNG society, and in essence it's not bad one. It's similar to the 'eye-for-an-eye' or 'tooth-for-a-tooth' doctrine. You could, of course, call it 'revenge', or you could call it 'paying your dues'. Applied in some circumstances, it would seem the fair and moral thing to demand. I am not an anthropologist, so I'm certainly not going to examine the payback principle any more deeply. Except as it applies to pigs and visiting BBC film crews. Basically, we were advised that if we ran over a pig, the owner would demand, at the very least, that we pay him back a similar animal. BBC film crews are not in the habit of packing spare pigs amongst the camera gear, and even the most resourceful PA would have winced at having to ring Television Centre in London and ask them to 'Red Star over a couple of porkers'. And it's no good trying to negotiate – offering a bagful of pork sausages or a tin of luncheon meat certainly won't work. They want a live pig. And they want it now. If you can't provide the pig, you may find yourself up in front of the village court and committed to providing 'services in lieu', up to the value of the pig. Possibly a few years' worth! This could definitely disrupt your shooting schedule! I may sound as if I'm being a trifle frivolous about it now, but then it's years later and I'm safe in London. Believe me, back in PNG in 1983 the prospect of pig payback was a great incentive to drive very carefully and very slowly, or – if you did hit a pig – very fast indeed. Either way, driving across New Guinea wasn't a relaxing experience.

Neither was flying, in tiny little planes whose pilots assured us (assured?) that normal navigation instruments were useless in the jungly mountains, and that the only way to land on the pocket-handkerchief-sized runways deep in the forest was to 'wait for a gap in the clouds and go for it'. Nevertheless, always overloaded, and often hours late, we eventually arrived safely at wherever the next location was. And the next location was …

… Baier River Sanctuary. By this stage Laura was overcoming her phobias about cars and planes. Obviously, she needed to move on to the next phase of the confrontation therapy. Bring on the insects. The Baier River Sanctuary was actually designed to protect various birds and animals but, in practice, you could have been forgiven for believing that it was principally an insect reserve. Even going up the drive to the sanctuary buildings involved breaking through a 30-foot-long spider's web, festooned with hundreds of hand-sized spiders. Inside the buildings, the conditions seemed to have been specially designed to make creepy-crawlies feel at home. It was dark and damp – the perfect habitat for cockroaches and beetles. And didn't they know it? New Guinea insects don't so much scuttle as lumber, since they tend to be at least four times the size of normal insects.

'At least,' I tried to reassure Laura, 'you can see them coming!'

See them? You could *hear* them, clomping around under the beds or dragging themselves in and out of the bread bins. 'OK they're big,' I admitted, 'but I promise you they are totally harmless. Believe me, none of these creatures can in any way hurt you,' I told Laura.

Unfortunately, nobody seemed to have told the locals. When I called up a couple of the sanctuary staff and asked them please to clear our room of cockroaches, they ran off screaming!

Maybe I'd failed to make myself properly understood. This was a recurring problem, as, frankly, I was having a lot of trouble with the language. Most people in PNG speak pidgin English which, in theory at least, ought to be fairly easy to grasp. But I couldn't. Brian Finch had run me through a basic vocabulary back in Port Moresby, but though it seemed perfectly clear when he spoke it in his measured Sussex accent, it sounded like a complete gabble coming from anyone else. At least at Baier River I had a chance for a little relaxed study. There was a notice in the toilet. On the notice, were lots of little drawings, depicting a man dropping his trousers, using the loo, and flushing it. This was not graffiti. They were precise instructions on toilet usage, for those more used to going *au naturel* out in the jungle. Having got used to going that way myself over the previous days, I was quite grateful for the reminder. I was also grateful for the language lesson: the instructions were written in pidgin English. The heading – in large capital letters – was:

'GUTPELA PASIM BELONG YUSIM HAUS PEK PEK.'

Having plenty of time, I sat there kicking away the cockroaches and translating. So – just in case you ever find yourself in a similar situation – here comes 'How to speak Pidgin', Lesson One:

The basic principle of pidgin English is that it is English that has been passed on down the generations by people who don't naturally speak it. In a sense, I suppose, it's English spoken with a very heavy local accent, in this case New Guinean. Inevitably, over the years some of the words have got misheard or misspelt, and have eventually become almost unrecognizable, especially when they're written down. It always reminds me a bit of George Bernard Shaw's original 'script' for *Pygmalion* (the one that became *My Fair Lady*). Shaw wrote down Eliza Doolittle's cockney accent 'phonetically'. This was meant to help the actress get it right. In fact, it merely demonstrated what a patronizing, pedantic old blighter Shaw was. All he really needed to do was put in an instruction, 'Please do this in a broad cockney accent', and I'm sure most actresses would have obliged. As it was, they needed a translator to work out what he was on about. Well, I know I did. When we had to read out Shaw in class at school, I used to find it totally unintelligible. The teacher had to explain it all to us. '*Garn wiv ya*' is 'Go on with you' in cockney; '*A lurvely lie-dee*' is 'a lovely lady', and so on. Not at all dissimilar to pidgin English, really. I suppose that's why, as I sat on the loo at Baier River trying to figure out that notice, I started thinking of Julie Andrews.

So ... GUTPELA PASIM BELONG YUSIM HAUS PEK
PEK ... It seemed to translate literally like this:

GUTPELA: Good fellow. PASIM: Person. BELONG:
Belong. YUSIM: Use him. HAUS: House. PEK PEK: I
wasn't exactly sure of that one yet.

So the sentence seemed to read: 'Good fellow person
belong use him in house pek pek.'

Since the illustration depicted a man sitting on a
lavatory, I deduced (correctly, I'm sure) that 'pek pek' was
whatever he was depositing in the loo. Therefore, the
'house pek pek' was, to use a colloquial expression, 'the
shit house' (sorry it doesn't rhyme). The sentence still
wasn't exactly Shakespeare (or even Shaw), but I was
getting the idea. A 'good fellow person' is a 'good bloke'. I
seemed to recall something about a pidgin English report
of a royal visit to PNG which mentioned 'Gutpela pasim
numba wonne sone belong Missi Qwin'. This referred to
Prince Charles, and translated roughly as: That admirable
fellow the Queen's number one son. (By the way, any
pidgin English experts reading this ... please don't write in
and tell me I've got a few syllables wrong. I'm sure I have,
but I'm doing my best.) So, back to the loo. 'Gutpela pasim
belong yusim haus pek pek' seemed to translate basically
as 'A good bloke is he who uses the toilet.' Quite a
philosophical thought, really. The definition of a good
chap is one who goes to the lav. What an optimistic take
on life! If only it were true; what a wonderful world it
would be. Obviously philanthropy wasn't the point of this
notice. It was purely practical. Basically all it was saying
was: 'Look, you may have been in the habit of dumping
behind a bush out there in the jungle, but it's making an
awful mess of the garden, so would you mind using this

nice new-fangled toilet, and, in case you've never seen one before, this is what you do.'

Anyway, I hope you find that little lesson in pidgin useful if you ever go to PNG. I would just add one serious word of warning. And the word is 'puk puk'. This is another pidgin English word, and it means … Well, what do you think it means? 'Puk puk.' Chicken, perhaps? Wrong. A puk puk is a crocodile. So puk puk and pek pek. Very similar, and yet very different indeed. But obviously the possibility of their getting mixed up is very real, and could be very unfortunate. Put it this way: if you happen to be visiting Port Moresby Zoo, and you get 'caught short', for Heaven's sake *don't* go into the 'Haus Puk Puk' and drop your trousers. I mean, OK, you could claim 'payback' from the zookeeper, but some things are irreplaceable.

Actually, whilst we're wallowing in pek pek stories, my favourite is this:

Some years ago, a big American film company were shooting a jungle-adventure-type film on location in New Guinea. The story centred round a giant man-eating crocodile which was terrorizing the local tribes. The climactic scene would be where the 'great-white-hunter' hero faced the evil beast and slew it, thus earning the gratitude of the local tribesmen. The great white hunter was played by an American star actor. The local tribesmen were to be played by real local tribesmen. It wasn't going to be a demanding role for them, because all they had to do was run away from the crocodile screaming with fear. So, came the day to shoot the big scene. Everything was set up. A masterpiece of logistics, involving hundreds of tribesmen. Hopefully, it would be a one-take job. But alas, no. Given the signal to come screaming out of the jungle, the tribesmen didn't so much panic as saunter. Instead of looking terrified, they smiled and chatted as if they were taking an afternoon stroll.

'For God's sake,' yelled the director, waving at them frantically, 'you're being chased by a goddam man-eating monster!'

The tribesmen merely smiled and waved back at him. Then someone suggested that maybe the problem was that the locals didn't really understand what the director was talking about. They didn't speak English (let alone American). 'So what *do* they speak?' he demanded. 'Pidgin,' came the answer. The solution was obvious. On the next take, they'd get the leader of the fleeing tribesmen to yell out: 'Help! Help! We're being chased by a giant crocodile' (in pidgin), and the locals would understand such motivation and panic accordingly. However, this vital line couldn't possibly be entrusted to a 'native' (anyway, he'd probably demand a whole sty full of pigs if he had a speaking part). So an American actor donned arse grass and got himself 'blacked up' to play the part. All he needed now was his line. So what was pidgin for 'crocodile'? 'Pok pok', was it? 'Pik pik'? Something like that. Then someone remembered the correct word ... or *did* they? I dare say you can guess what happened. Remember, 'puk puk' is crocodile, and 'pek pek' ... isn't.

They set up the scene again. The cameras rolled. Our hero leaps into shot. In races the leader of the tribesmen, looking suitably terrified.

'What's going on?' demands our hero. The leading tribesman yells out the answer:

'Help! Help! We're being chased by a giant pek pek!'

Result: out of the jungle stagger rank upon rank of fearsome-looking tribesmen, howling with laughter! Sounds like one for *It'll Be Alright on the Night* to me! Mind you, it sounds like a much scarier idea for a film, too. A giant pek pek!

But enough of these scatological digressions ... what about the birds? The truth is that I didn't really see very many at Baier River. Neither did we succeed in filming that much. As it turned out, this set the tone for much of the trip. I *heard* a scrabbling in the undergrowth that was probably a pitta. I saw the display ground of the truly amazing Blue Bird of Paradise (was that one sponsored by an Australian, I wonder: who *was* this 'Blue' bloke?), but I didn't see the bird. Apparently, it is simply dazzling, and it also makes an incredible electronic-sounding buzzing noise that has to be heard to be believed. I'm not sure I believe it, 'cos I didn't hear it, either.

I was actually prevented from seeing a Yellow-breasted Bowerbird by Richard, the producer. How's this for frustration? We were taken to the bower, and for an hour or so I did 'pieces to camera' explaining how 'this extraordinary arch-shaped construction is not a nest but is the male's way of showing off to the female'. I pointed out how 'the bird decorates the whole thing with all manner of coloured berries, and how the pair mate on the bower, but then the female goes off to build a nest, lays eggs and rears the chicks all on her own.' 'What a fascinating bird it is,' I enthused ... 'and what a pity we can't actually see one!' At which point I noticed that Richard was gesticulating at me, indicating that I was on no account to turn round. I tried not to let the confusion show in my eyes, and kept burbling on about 'beautiful bowerbirds'. Two minutes later, Richard said 'Cut'. Of course, I immediately whipped round to see what was going on behind me. There seemed to be nothing. In fact, I only really discovered the truth when I got back to England and saw the 'rushes'. What had actually happened was that, even as I was raving on about him, the male Yellow-breasted Bowerbird had sneaked into the back of the shot, plonked a few more berries in his bower, hopped up and down, almost waved to the camera, and sneaked off again! Richard explained that he hadn't wanted me to turn round 'cos I might have scared it away, and anyway, 'it looked quite funny!' Oh sure. Big laugh. Especially 'cos, even though I waited by the bower for the rest of the day, it never came back. So can I tick a bird I was in the same shot with but didn't actually see? OK. I know the answer ... 'Oh, pek pek,' is all I can say.

The people who ran the Baier River Sanctuary were lovely and, in a slightly masochistic way, I wouldn't have missed staying there for the world. I'm sure the wildlife can be wonderful but, frankly, we weren't very lucky, not least with the weather, which was consistently dank and dark. As it happens, the sleeping arrangements weren't exactly conducive to honeymoon-type activities either, as we all had to share a sort of temporary dormitory, where privacy was only achieved by erecting screens of table-tennis tables. So, all in all, I have to confess that I wasn't really very sad to leave, and I'm sure Laura would second that. Nevertheless, I was a little taken aback when she greeted the news that we were next going to go filming 'up a mountain' with a somewhat non-committal shrug: 'Oh yes? That sounds nice.' She had learnt to be sceptical ... and she was right.

I liked the sound of going up a mountain. So far, we'd been in the lowlands, and it had been pretty gloomy. I fancied some bracing mountain air and some wide open spaces. Well ... there no doubt *are* mountains like that in New Guinea, but Mount Missim wasn't one of them. We arrived in the area at about five o'clock in the afternoon. It was absolutely bucketing down. We were met by our local 'contacts', a young American couple, Steve and Melinda. They had been in the area for some time, studying some of the birds that lived up on the mountain. Steve and Melinda themselves lived at the bottom of the mountain, in a spacious comfortable house with lots of cosy bedrooms with big double beds in them. I liked the look of it very much. However, connubial canoodlings were not on the BBC's schedule.

We were in fact supposed to climb up the mountain that afternoon and ensconce ourselves in the temporary camp at the top, which was Steve and Melinda's base for field work. It was going to be a long and arduous climb. It would take at least three hours and we were already two hours late. This meant that it would be dark long before we reached the top. It was also raining very hard indeed. We all stood there getting wetter and wetter. There was a team of local porters to carry the cameras, sound equipment and some very heavy lights that would be needed for filming in murky jungle; there were Neil and Joel checking the gear; and there was Beth still writing up notes on a waterproof pad. There was Richard discussing the situation with Steve and Melinda; and there were Laura and I awaiting the outcome. It soon became clear that there was some debate – and possibly disagreement – about whether it was worth – or maybe even wise – setting off so late in the day in such awful conditions.

I could see the dilemma. Richard had a schedule to keep to and there was no guarantee that the weather would be any better the next day. Steve, on the other hand, seemed loath to demand that the porters (whom he had hired) should make such an arduous climb largely in the dark, particularly as they would also want to come back down again that night to sleep in their own village. For my part, I was still casting glances towards the cosy house across the road. As it turned out, I was the first to snap. 'We're not going,' I announced. 'There's no point. I know perfectly well we won't shoot anything with me for ages. I'll just be sitting there waiting. We can come up first thing tomorrow morning.' I presumed Laura agreed with me. Richard didn't. It may well have been my chickening out that spurred him on to be instantly intrepid. In any event, he immediately countered my decision by setting off up the path and exhorting the rest of the crew to follow. To be fair, I could see it from his angle, and indeed I think he saw it from mine. 'OK. See you tomorrow,' he called back. Steve and Melinda quickly decided they would split forces. Melinda would accompany the porters and the crew, while Steve would stay back at the house with us. I couldn't help suspecting that he was relieved, and she was envious. However, it soon became clear that Steve was also concerned.

That evening, we enjoyed a lovely meal and a chat in what were by far the most comfortable conditions we'd so far experienced in PNG. But, as time went on, I noticed Steve kept glancing at his watch. Eventually, at about ten o'clock, he said: 'I'm just going to drive over to the village and make sure the porters have got back OK.' He was gone for an hour or so. When he returned, he was clearly worried. 'No, they still aren't back.' 'So what could have happened to them?' I asked. 'Well, probably nothing.' Steve tried to reassure us and himself. 'It really is an awful night out there and there's no moon, so it'll be very dark. They may well have decided to stay up at the camp. Obviously, they know the mountain very well.'

I sensed that what Steve meant by this remark was that you *needed* to know the mountain very well, otherwise it could be a dangerous place, especially if you were wandering around on it on a pitch-dark stormy night. Some time around midnight Laura and I retired to the first double bed of our honeymoon. Not only double, it was also a waterbed, which was a new experience altogether! Slurpy but fun. (Describes the whole thing really, doesn't it?!) We slept deeply, woken only briefly by the sound of the front door opening or shutting. I suspected that Steve had not been able to rest so easily.

Next morning the sun streamed in through our windows and I woke early. I pottered round the garden trying to identify honey-eaters on the blossoms, and thinking 'this is more like it'. PNG wasn't so grim after all. Laura wandered out on to the balcony with a cup of fresh coffee, and she agreed. Then we heard Steve's vehicle turning into the drive. We suddenly felt quite nervous. 'So what's happened? Any news?'

'Yes. It's OK. The porters got back in the early hours. It took them a lot longer to get up because the trail was so slippery, and then they stayed at the camp for some food, and hoping the weather might improve, so it was pretty late before they set off back. But the crew's up there safely, and the porters are all back safely. Well, except one bloke, who apparently got ill. He went back to the camp, so presumably he'll come back down today. Anyway ... we'd better get going.'

Steve was clearly relieved, though perhaps not completely so yet. Maybe he'd feel better when we got to the top. Meanwhile, before then, we were going to feel a whole lot worse! The thing about a lot of New Guinea mountains is that they are covered in rain forest. And the thing about rain forest is that a) it's a forest, full of trees; and b) it rains ... a lot.

OK, it wasn't actually raining as we climbed but the trail was still as slippery as ice. As it got steeper – and it got very steep – for every step you took forward, you tended to slide back a couple. And this was where the trees became a hazard. Well, not the trees themselves, but their roots. Some of them curled across the path like glistening snakes intent on tripping us, while others grew upwards out of the soil (as mangroves grow out of mud) so that if we'd fallen on them, we would have been impaled on their spikes. I simply cannot exaggerate what an unpleasant trek it was up Mount Missim. It took us four hours, and by the time we reached the top Laura and I were exhausted and literally in tears (and I do mean both of us). Even Steve, who had done the climb masses of times, in no way pretended it was fun. But obviously he had other things on his mind. As soon as we reached the camp and saw Melinda, the first thing Steve asked was: 'Is the porter all right?'

Her answer obviously distressed him. 'What porter?'

The camp was not cosy (especially not when compared with the house and the waterbed). It consisted of a large square of earth covered by a rather leaky tarpaulin roof which (almost) sheltered the cooking area and the sleeping quarters; that is, the half-dozen sleeping-bags that lay side by side at night but which, by day, were hung up on the washing-line, drying out after being constantly dripped on. (From one waterbed to another!) The area round the campsite had been cleared of trees and, every now and then, you were reminded why. There would suddenly be a noise rather like a cross between a huge creaking door, an elephant's trumpeting, and a small explosion, followed by a shrieking bird and then an eerie silence. This was the sound of falling trees. The forest is so damp that the timber gets rotten, and every now and again a tree literally keels over. It was disconcerting to hear, and equally disconcerting to see, especially when it happened on the edge of the clearing. I was grateful that somebody had done their mathematics, as none of the massive trunks actually fell on the campsite itself.

One thing I'd been right about; if we *had* gone up on the previous evening with the crew, I certainly would have been just sitting around waiting. We hadn't arrived at the camp till nearly midday, but even by then they hadn't been able to film anything at all. This was mainly because, even with the sun out, it was still extremely gloomy in the forest so that it was necessary to set up artificial lights, which in some cases would have to be buried or camouflaged. It was going to be some time before the camera turned over – especially as it was now raining again. For the rest of the day we sat huddled under the tarpaulin. So did the PNG insects. They're not daft. Insects don't enjoy getting soaked any more than humans, so we shared the relative dryness of our camp with the usual assortment of monster beetles, spiders and cockroaches. We each had our different ways of discouraging them. Laura would shoo them away, I would kick them, and Neil and Joel ate them! Yes, that's right. They assured us that insects were full of protein and had rather a nice crunchy toffee-like texture, and that the local people ate them all the time. The couple of local people we had with us didn't seem to share the taste, and merely laughed in disbelief as Neil munched on a beetleburger.

To tell the truth, though I may make light of it now, the atmosphere up there on the mountain was strangely unnerving. In fact, it was positively spooky. It was incredibly gloomy. It was also disconcertingly quiet – 'Too quiet', as they say in the movies. For much of the time nobody spoke. We just sat there reading or gazing at the rain. Sometimes Steve and Melinda would whisper to each other. I assumed they were worrying over what had happened to the missing porter. If the silence was broken, it would be by the crashing of another tree, or by what sounded disturbingly like a burst of machine-gun fire. I knew full well this was only the call of the Rifle Bird, but I never really got used to it. I mean, as if things weren't weird enough, it sounded like we were about to be attacked by armed guerrillas. And talking of being attacked ... if there *were* still cannibals and head-hunters in PNG, surely this was where they'd be? We experienced a definite feeling of tension, of being stuck up there in the 'unknown'. It was bad enough by day. At night it was worse. Especially if you wanted to slip off to the loo.

This was a real test of nerves. This particular haus pek pek certainly didn't need any instructions telling you how to use it. It was primitive in the extreme, being merely a deep hole with a few planks and a precarious plastic toilet seat over it. The poet who insulted the lovely Port Moresby sewage farm should have reserved his little rhyme for this set-up. This was indeed a shit pit. Perhaps mercifully, it had been excavated about fifty yards away from the camp. But unmercifully it was in an area that had not been cleared of soggy old trees. Thus going to the toilet in the middle of the night was as scary a journey as I have ever had to undertake. You wriggled out of your soggy sleeping-bag, staggered through pitch-dark jungle – wondering if a cannibal was about to leap out on you – fumbled your way onto the seat, and then sat there praying that a rotten tree wouldn't fall on your head and hammer you down into a pit full of pek pek! If it didn't, you staggered back to the camp and crawled back into your sleeping-bag, only to discover it had been taken over by a giant cockroach.

And this was our honeymoon.

We were also meant to be filming birds. And the particular bird we were hoping to film on Mount Missim was the MacGregor's Bowerbird. Was MacGregor the discoverer or the patron? I dunno, but it makes a change to have a Scottish name instead of some mid-European royal person, doesn't it? Anyway, like most bowerbirds, MacGregor's impresses by what it does, rather than what it looks like (though it does have a little surprise in the plumage department, as I shall eventually relate). The bird is hardly bigger then a starling, and is sort of olive-brown all over except for a barely visible streak of orange on the top of its head, hardly as conspicuous as the crown stripe on a Goldcrest (or Kinglet, if you want the American equivalent). Basically, MacGregor's Bowerbird is not impressive, but its bower certainly is. It builds a maypole several feet high by weaving small twigs up a thin sapling. Which is easier said than done – for a person, let alone a small bird. What's more, it clears a sort of moat round the maypole, which it then neatly carpets with moss. This is, of course, intended to impress a female bowerbird. It also impressed me, and indeed the rest of the crew as they prepared for filming. The first thing they had to do was secrete a couple of lights amongst nearby foliage to illuminate the bower, which the bird had inconsiderately built in a very dark part of the forest. Then Neil supervised the construction of a hide, which in this case resembled a small igloo built of leaves, with a little hole for the camera lens to poke through. It was OK, but not as impressive as the bower. Of course, getting film of the bower was easy enough, and it was equally easy to film me rattling on about what an amazing construction it was. This I duly did. No doubt Richard was hoping that the bird would sneak into the shot behind my back, as the Yellow-breasted Bowerbird had done. But MacGregor's had no such intention of upsetting me. In fact, as it turned out, MacGregor's was on my side.

It was also extremely camera-shy. Neil was, of course, hoping to film the display, and maybe even a pair mating. For hour after hour he sat in the hide, camera poised, finger on the button. Nothing. Then, half-way through the second day, I saw him wandering disconsolately back to camp to have a cup of tea. I asked if I could go and sit in the hide whilst he was away. No sooner had I settled down and peeped through the view-hole, than in hopped MacGregor's Bowerbird. I suppose I should have raced back to camp and got Neil. But then if I'd left the hide, I would almost certainly have frightened off the bird, wouldn't I? Anyway, I had a feeling this bird was here to entertain *me*, not show off for the camera. And entertain me he did. At first, he seemed to be merely popping in to repair his maypole. He adjusted a few twigs, and stood back to admire his work. Then he seemed to pause for a moment, as if thinking he'd maybe heard a passing female. Suddenly he decided he 'might as well give it a go'. He started to hop round his little moat. Faster and faster he went. Then he began to leap up and down, and finally, suddenly, as the climax of his act ... he burst into flames! Well, that was the effect. That little orange streak on his head, hitherto almost invisible, suddenly fanned out into a dazzling crown of bright orange that lit up his murky little circus ring. He certainly didn't need any artificial illumination. He was wearing his own spotlight right on top of his head. I nearly applauded. Apparently, though, it didn't impress the ladies and no female appeared. With a shake and a shrug, he retracted his crest, had a quick preen, and disappeared back into the gloom.

At which point Neil returned from his tea-break. For two more days he sat in the hide. But MacGregor's Bowerbird never came back.

While Neil continued his lonely vigil, I went wandering with my binoculars in the damp, dark forest. I remember thinking it was rather like going birding in a car-wash. Except I reckoned I would have seen more birds in a car-wash. As it turned out, I broke my record for the longest time I've ever gone outdoors without actually seeing a bird. I *heard* a couple of squeaks, but I *saw* nothing at all during a three-hour walk in the forest. That's right. Three hours – nothing. And yet isn't rain forest supposed to support the richest variety of avifauna of all habitats? Yes indeed, and indeed it does. But, as I'm sure anyone who's birded in such places would confirm, it can also seem incredibly devoid of life. There are really two reasons for this. One is that most of the action is going on right up in the very top canopy of extremely tall trees, where you can't see it and can barely hear it, and the other is that many of the birds travel in feeding flocks or 'waves'. Every now and then you may find yourself in the midst of such a wave, and suddenly the trees are alive with so many birds of so many species that you tend to panic and not know where to look. Then, as quickly as the wave had come, it's gone again, and the jungle reverts to emptiness. The trick is to take in a mental picture of as many of the different birds as you can and look them up in the book later. You'll often be astonished by how many you saw, and how many you still can't identify! In fact, a rain-forest bird-wave is a thrilling experience. But the only wave we saw on Mount Missim was the one we got from the crew, as Laura and I left them to try and get some decent bird pictures, whilst we set off back down the mountain, bound for a small hotel on a small island, and maybe even a small honeymoon.

Laura and I were happy to leave Mount Missim. We'd never really felt safe there somehow. In fact, just how close to danger we had been we only discovered several days later. We'd thoroughly enjoyed a relaxing weekend on the delightful little desert-island retreat of Loloata, a short boat ride from Port Moresby, but seemingly miles from the city and its rascals. This had been all arranged by Brian Finch. When we returned to the capital, we met up with him so we could take him out for a 'thank you' supper. We were surprised when he told us that the film crew would be joining us. We hadn't thought they were due back for a couple of days. Indeed, they weren't, but, as things had turned out, they'd had to leave Mount Missim in a bit of a hurry. So what had happened?

Apparently, the day after we had left the mountain, the missing porter had been found ... dead. He was lying in the jungle not many yards from the trail and only half a mile or so from the campsite. Foul play was not suspected. It seems that on the climb up the mountain that night he had complained of feeling unwell. After a rest he had declared himself fit enough to go back down to the village with the rest of the team. However, shortly after setting off again, he had almost collapsed and was clearly running some kind of fever. He decided – or was advised by his friends – to return to the camp. I couldn't help musing about how caring his friends were that they had let him go back alone, but presumably they had thought that because it wasn't far, he'd be OK. No doubt also, on a dark and stormy night, they were anxious to get back home themselves as quickly as possible. Anyway, he never made it. It seemed likely that he had become disorientated, wandered off the path, and collapsed. No one knew how long he'd survived. Probably he'd died that night, from 'natural causes' – likely to have been some fatal illness, rather than 'exposure'. True, it was wet and nasty on the mountain and, once you have lost the trail, it is very hard to get your bearings, but if the man had survived till morning, he would surely have been able to call for help or managed to reorient himself. Had he been found a long way from camp, one would have had to conclude that he had endured the nightmare of wandering lost in the jungle until his strength had finally given way. As it was, he was so close to help and safety that his death seemed all the more tragic, albeit that it must surely have been fairly quick.

Obviously, everyone in the camp was stunned and upset by what had happened. They were also frightened. Remember I explained the PNG principle of 'payback'? An eye for an eye, a tooth for a tooth, a pig for a pig ... or – was it now to be a porter for a porter? Or to put it even more chillingly, a life for a life. It did not matter that the porter had died of 'natural' causes, payback could still apply.

Within a few hours, it was clear that it did. Melinda, the American scientist, had been walking close to the campsite when a man suddenly leapt out of the jungle, grabbed her round the neck, and put a machete to her throat. Rather than panic instantly, she'd had the control – and no doubt

the awareness of New Guinea lore – to ask 'Why?' The
answer was simply: 'This is the New Guinea way.' No
doubt it didn't seem the moment for an anthropological
debate. Melinda screamed, and, fortunately, her attacker
melted back into the jungle whence he had come. Melinda
raced back to the camp, where she and Steve explained
the situation to the film crew. The porter's family or tribe,
on hearing of his death, would have immediately discussed
who was to 'blame'. They had obviously come to the
conclusion that it was Steve or Melinda, since they had
hired the porters in the first place, and were therefore
responsible for their safety. It seemed that the life of the
porter would have to be 'paid back' with the life of either
Steve or Melinda. That this was no idle conjecture had
already been shown.

You may well yourself be thinking that this appor-
tioning of blame was not really fair. And I'd agree with
you. If I'd still been on the mountain at that time, I'm sure
I would have been asking: 'Why wasn't it the other
porters' fault (his so-called friends) for letting him walk
back alone?' I have to confess I would also have been hard
put to defend the BBC for dragging everyone up there in
the first place. I mean, Heaven knows I don't want to be
disloyal to my producer, but he had insisted they went up
that evening, though, of course, he'd had no idea that
anything awful was going to happen. Actually, the truth is
that, if I *had* been still up on the mountain, I would not
have been indulging in hypothetical arguments. I'd've been
getting the hell out of there! I do suspect, though, that I
would have been racing down the trail yelling, 'It's not my
fault. Take Richard!'

Anyway … that's exactly what everyone had done – got
the hell out of there, I mean. They had buried most of the
heavy lighting and camera gear, and hurried back down
while it was still daylight. The next day they had returned

with some kind of armed guard, rescued the equipment, and flown back to Port Moresby, where they were now relating the whole scary tale to Laura and myself. But what of Steve and Melinda? They had presumably been left at their home, in fear for their lives. Naturally, we kept in touch with them during the rest of our stay in PNG, and after we had returned to England. Fortunately, they had earned so much local respect, and indeed gratitude (for providing work in the area), that there was a general feeling of outrage that Melinda had been attacked, and certainly no animosity towards them. Nevertheless, they would not be out of danger until the whole affair had been discussed by the regional 'council', and their names officially cleared. In time this is exactly what happened, and, as it turned out, no payback was demanded at all. Nevertheless, Steve wrote to me saying that for many weeks they were extremely fearful that some friend or relation of the dead porter might decide to take the law into his own hands. They stayed on, studying the birds on Mount Missim, for a year or more after the event, but never again did they feel safe enough to sleep up at the campsite unguarded, or wander around as freely as they had done. I last heard that they were still researching happily in some other country. I hope they feel safer.

For the final week of our assignment Laura, I, and the film crew migrated south to a wonderful coastal wildlife reserve, Bensbach, which was more closely related in landscape and wildlife, to northern Australia. This wasn't surprising, since the Northern Territory is but a short flap away across the Torres Strait. We filmed Aussie specialities, such as wallabies, and kookaburras, and blokes with enormous bellies and corks hanging from their hats. There were also masses of water birds, but the warden of the reserve had a disconcerting habit of tazzing straight at them in his speedboat and then wondering why they flew off, rather than sit there to be filmed. Richard ended up having to edit in some of the stuff from the shit pit!

It was very pleasant at Bensbach, and frankly, a great relief from the murk and damp of the forest. But we really couldn't forget the Mount Missim incident. It seemed to confirm a rather disturbing conclusion about this trip in particular and – more to the point – about PNG in general. PNG was, and still is, quite a dangerous country. I don't just mean the rascals, though apparently the problem of crime has escalated and spread well beyond the capital city. What I really mean is that, unless visitors understand and respect the culture and customs of the place, then they are at risk. What's more, as I said at the beginning of this chapter, I do believe that, ironically, television can exacerbate the problem by making such places seem familiar and safe. Certainly my little mini-series ended up that way. It didn't include the bank manager tribesman, and it didn't include the scary drives in torrential rain wondering what would happen to us if we broke down miles from anywhere, and it certainly didn't include the death on Mount Missim. Looking back now, I can't help thinking we took a lot of risks, and may have been in even more danger than we realized. So why weren't we more aware at the time? Well, let me put it this way: if watching wildlife and travel programmes can make you blasé, I suspect making them may make you more so. Maybe it's a sort of extension of 'camera blindness', as though being with a film crew gives you some sort of immunity. I often wonder what would we have said if we had been captured by cannibals? 'Sorry, you can't eat us, were from the BBC!'

In any event, I rather regret that this element of our PNG experience wasn't referred to in the final film. What it *did* include was lots of beautiful birds. Some of which I actually saw, but quite a few of which were cut in from 'library film', often shot many years ago. There was even a sequence of MacGregor's Bowerbird doing its fire dance. On the commentary, I muttered something about 'how lucky we are to see the display,' and 'sorry the film is all a bit dark and grainy, but there wasn't very much light in the jungle.' The truth is that it had been shot by an Australian cameraman just after the war, and the film was 'dark and grainy' because it was 40 years old and held together with Sellotape! There were also masses of lovely close-ups of birds of paradise. Some of them were in cages, and some came from David Attenborough films (I wonder if he actually saw them either!), but some of them I really did see, and they were wonderfully filmed and recorded by Neil and Joel.

In fact, I must give all credit to everyone on the crew. OK, there were 'cheats' in what the viewers finally saw on the screen, but, believe me, there are in most wildlife films, and in three weeks in a rain forest you're lucky to get anything except wet! Richard actually did a splendid job. I think my only real complaint would be that they decided to call it *Oddie in Paradise*! Ironic, or what?

I'd have gone for *Honeymoon in Hell*.

Outroduction

It's always a problem knowing when to stop ... writing a book I mean. In the case of this one, I just kept going until circumstances took me away from the word processor. As it happens, I had to go off to Spain to co-lead a trip round the Pyrenees, in search of several species that should have been there, but weren't. When I got back, I actually wanted to write about what had just happened – or rather, not happened! But when I looked at the list of other places and events I'd promised myself to cover, I realized there were much more magnificent 'dip outs' available. Several 'press trips' for a start, organized for journalists – which I can be when necessary – usually by Tourist Boards who don't appreciate that it really makes quite a lot of difference what time you go to certain places. Like, you *don't* go to Iceland in September – when it's empty! – or the Coto Donana in December – when it's cold and wet – or try to do the Galapagos in four days! All three of which I did. They were all frustrating, but I suspect they'd make rather good chapters! Then again, there were the good ones: gripping yarns, from Hong Kong in April to Flamborough Head in October. The fact is, I reckon I've actually got quite enough stuff to write another book immediately. But don't tell the publishers that! I've told them I need to go off on some more travels to gather more material. So that's really why I'm stopping this book now.

Hope you enjoyed 'the stories so far'.

Bye. And good birding.

What *is* He On About?
A Glossary of Birding Terms

There are some birding terms that I haven't been able to stop myself using in this book. The most frequent are:

TWITCHER

A bird-watcher obsessed with seeing rare birds, who is willing to travel long distances to tick them off on his or her list. A twitcher is said to 'twitch' a particular species (e.g. 'I twitched the Red-throated Pipit'). When many twitchers are gathered in one place, to see one bird, the event constitutes a 'twitch'.

DIP OUT

To fail to see the bird you wanted to see (e.g. 'I dipped out on the Red-throated Pipit').

TO BE GRIPPED OFF

To fail to see a rare bird, which others have seen (e.g. 'My friend Bob gripped me off with the Red-throated Pipit', i.e. Bob saw it, I didn't).

TO STRING

To mis-identify a bird and not realize it (or at least not admit it). The bird and the bird-watcher are both said to be 'stringy' (e.g. 'The Red-throated Pipit was stringy. And so is Bob!' Or – to put it another way – 'Bob is a stringer').

For a fuller explanation of these and many other esoteric matters, I can only immodestly refer you to *Bill Oddie's Little Black Bird Book*, soon to republished by Robson Books. Have they *no* shame?

NB
Practical experience of any of these terms is *not essential to the enjoyment of this book*!